Amy Hemmert and Tammy Pelstring

The Laptop Lunch User's Guide

Fresh Ideas for Making Wholesome, Earth-Friendly Lunches Your Kids Will Love

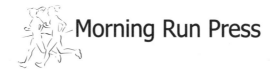

Morning Run Press

Credits

Content Editor:	Jodi Godfrey Meisler, M.S., R.D.
Copy Editor:	N. Ann Chenoweth, Ph.D.
Photography:	Obentec, Inc.
Cover Design:	Janet Allinger
Illustrations:	Gary Hathaway

Morning Run Press
849 Almar Avenue, Suite C-323
Santa Cruz, CA 95060 USA

www.morningrunpress.com

ISBN 0-9719453-0-6

With love to our kids: Phoenix, Brian, Dana, and Triton

Table of Contents

Acknowledgements

We are grateful to the following people for their help in producing this book:

Jodi Godfrey Meisler, M.S., R.D. for her thoughtful comments and in-depth knowledge of family nutrition.

N. Ann Chenoweth, Ph.D. for her careful editing and invaluable feedback.

Gary Hathaway for his fine illustrations.

Janet Allinger for her artistic cover design.

Nancy Rapp and her team of expert printers for their patience and expertise.

Gateway School for allowing us to participate in the implementation of their waste-free lunch program.

The parents who field-tested our recipes and provided feedback.

The moms and dads who distributed and/or responded to our surveys.

Robert W. Lindeman, Ph.D. for his invaluable input, his technical assistance, and his inimitable wit.

The various organizations and individuals who have educated us along the way.

The Mikes for their support and understanding.

Our kids, Phoenix, Brian, Dana, and Triton, for their inspiring words and deeds.

A Note to Our Readers

The aim of this book is to provide general health and nutrition information for families with children. The information supplied herein is intended to complement, not substitute for, the advice of your own health care providers. Before making dietary changes, consult a health care provider who knows your family and is familiar with your needs.

It is not our intention to give a detailed account of all the information that is publicly available concerning nutrition and waste reduction, but rather to provide information on how to make nutritionally sound, earth-friendly lunches for school-age children. If you are looking for a more in-depth treatment of the issues raised in this book, we encourage you to seek out other available resources and to learn as much as you can so that you can best satisfy your family's needs.

Every effort has been made to provide the most accurate and up-to-date information possible. Please be aware, however, that common beliefs and attitudes do change. Continue to educate yourself on these issues as they evolve, and remember to use this book as a general guide and not as your sole source of information on nutrition and waste reduction.

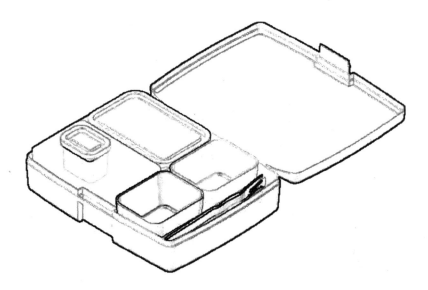

Introduction

Thank you for buying our book and for making the commitment to reduce lunchtime waste. By packing our children's lunches in reusable containers we, as parents, can greatly decrease the amount of trash dumped into our country's landfills while at the same time providing our children with nutritious meals.

When our children first started to attend elementary school, we became aware of the tremendous volume of trash generated in our schools, not only in classrooms, copy rooms, and offices, but also in school lunchrooms. If you walk around the lunchroom at your children's schools and take a good look at the lunches being eaten there, here's what you're likely to see:

◆ sandwiches sealed in disposable plastic bags
◆ fruits and vegetables in plastic bags
◆ chips, cookies, fruit bars, granola bars, cheeses, and fruit leathers in single-use packages
◆ single-serving yogurts, applesauces, and puddings in disposable plastic containers
◆ crackers, pretzels, chips, and other snack foods sealed in plastic bags
◆ disposable juice boxes, juice pouches, soda cans, water bottles, and milk cartons
◆ plastic forks and spoons
◆ paper napkins
◆ reusable lunchboxes and disposable paper and plastic bags

If we look at the amount of trash in just one child's lunch, multiply that by the number of school days in a year and then by the number of school-age children in the United States alone, we can see how much lunchtime trash American children generate annually. In fact, it has been estimated that on average a school-age child using a disposable lunch generates 67 pounds of waste per school year. That equates to 18,760 pounds of lunch waste for just one average-size elementary school.

Contrast this with a waste-free alternative:

- sandwiches and other main dishes, fresh fruit, fresh vegetables, and treats in a reusable lunch container
- cloth napkins
- stainless-steel forks and spoons
- reusable drink containers
- reusable lunchboxes

Clearly, in the second scenario very little trash is generated because foods are bought in bulk or in larger packages. The packaging is left at home for reuse or recycling. Food waste also decreases because with a reusable lunch container, children can re-pack uneaten food instead of dumping it, packaging and all, into the school trash can.

But that's not all. Prepackaged foods are extremely expensive compared to bulk foods or foods sold in larger containers. According to the Sierra Club, Americans pay more for food packaging than we pay our farmers to grow our food. By not purchasing heavily packaged foods we can greatly reduce the amount of money we spend each month.

And what about nutrition? In *The Family Nutrition Book,* Dr. William Sears, M.D. reminds us that nutritious eating is extremely important to our well-being. He says, "After years of observation, I became convinced that the children who ate the healthiest foods were the healthiest kids. They were sick less often, had fewer discipline problems, and achieved better in school. They not only had healthier bodies, they had healthier minds." Moreover, prepackaged foods tend to be nutritionally inferior to unprocessed whole foods, and that's where Laptop Lunches come in. Laptop Lunches provide parents with the tools they need to provide their children with healthier lunches without sacrificing convenience.

We are a society made up of people on the go, and our food choices reflect this lifestyle. As a group, we tend to choose foods based on their convenience or appearance rather than on their nutritional value. However, what many of us fail to realize is that we often end up paying for this luxury in other ways, for example, with more trips to the doctor, more meetings with teachers, and the added stress of dealing with discipline issues.

As parents of school age children, we have the greatest influence over the food choices our children make, and the eating habits that we instill in our children now are the habits that will most likely follow them into adulthood. Thus, we need to consider not only what type of eaters our younger children are now, but also what type of eaters we want them to be when they are teenagers and adults.

If you're like us, you don't have a lot of time at the beginning (or at the end) of the day for making elaborate lunches. Parents perform a delicate balancing act and sometimes adding one more responsibility to the day can send us over the edge. Our goal in providing you with this product is to lift the "lunchbox burden" by giving you the tools you need for a smooth transition to a smart lunch. With this attractive reusable container and user's guide full of lunch ideas, you too will enjoy packing healthier, waste-free lunches for your family.

So, get ready, get set, and get going! We hope your Laptop Lunch helps your family eat well, save money, and reduce waste.

Did you know...

The New York State Department of Environmental Conservation estimates that one student taking a disposable lunch to school every day will create 45-90 pounds of garbage per year?

From the Lunchbox to the Landfill

As Americans we have come to depend on the many convenience products that are available to us, especially those intended to be discarded after a single use. We think nothing of ordering a cup of coffee, which arrives in a paper coffee cup with a plastic lid, a paper heat guard, a wooden stirrer, a napkin, and perhaps a paper sugar packet and plastic cream container. When we cannot finish a restaurant meal, we ask to take it home in a disposable container.

This reliance on disposable containers is evident everywhere, especially in the school lunch room. Most parents pack lunch items in single-use plastic bags, aluminum foil, or wax paper, or they purchase single-serving items that come in their own disposable packages. One company has gone so far as to produce an entire lunch packed in a completely disposable lunch container. It comes in a plastic molded tray, which is wrapped in plastic and boxed in cardboard packaging. When the child is finished eating, the packaging is dumped into the school trash can and hauled off to the landfill or incinerator.

Admittedly, these products are extremely convenient, but what is the environmental cost to a country that relies so heavily on them? Landfills are full and overflowing. Incinerators pump contaminants into the air. Communities are battling over who will accept the nation's trash. We all enjoy the conveniences that a disposable society offers, but few of us are willing to allow new landfills and incinerators to be built in our own backyards.

For this reason, waste disposal facilities are being built farther and farther from the towns where the waste is generated. While this is desirable for many reasons, it is also extremely expensive. The city of Prattville, Alabama, for example, trucks its waste to a landfill over 100 miles from town, a practice not all that uncommon in the United States. Towns like this would benefit greatly by reducing the amount of waste they generate and by improving recycling and composting programs in the community. They would save hundreds of thousands of dollars a year, and reduce fuel emissions to boot.

The shortage of land is another cost-related problem for communities and individuals. New York City, for example, generates about 14,000 tons of garbage a day. Approximately half is sent to waste disposal facilities in New York and half is trucked to New Jersey where it is incinerated or sent to transfer stations and then on to landfills in other states. Because the demand for waste-disposal sites in the New York area is high and the supply relatively low, costs have been increasing steadily. Furthermore, the number of garbage trucks on the road has increased, and waste disposal companies are reporting that they must wait up to three hours to unload, driving the price up even higher. These cost increases are then passed on to individuals in the form of higher waste disposal fees or increased taxes.

In recent years, more and more communities have lost battles to keep waste disposal facilities out of their neighborhoods. In 1992, the U.S. Supreme Court ruled that states did not have the right to refuse waste from other areas. That's one reason Michigan has allowed Toronto to truck its waste over the border to a Detroit-area landfill. Many Michigan residents, unhappy about the increased truck traffic on their freeways, have advocated incineration as an alternative, but finding an appropriate site has been difficult. The Canadians, to their credit, are looking for ways to reduce landfill waste through improved composting and recycling programs.

These are but a few examples of the many problems that we, as a convenience-based society, must grapple with. Every community, no matter how small, deals with issues surrounding waste management and disposal. We need to do more than just haul our trash cans out to the curb once or twice a week. We need to take a minute to think about where our trash goes once it is picked up from the curb and hauled out of sight.

In our communities we need to make wise waste disposal decisions. How and where will our trash be transported? How will it be disposed of? How much can we afford to pay? How can we convince people to cut down on the amount of trash they generate? How can we implement effective recycling and composting programs?

In dealing with these very difficult questions, it has become apparent to many that we cannot continue to generate the amount of garbage we are now generating. We must reduce our reliance on disposable items, like packaging, because this way of life is unsustainable. We need to find ways to cut down on the amount of packaging we use, and we need to do it now. Every single piece of packaging that we refuse to buy can make a tremendous difference.

Childhood Obesity

Prepackaged, processed foods have had a negative impact not only on our environment, but on the health of our children as well. The processing of foods makes it easy for manufacturers to add sugar, salt, hydrogenated oils, fillers, and other nutritionally inferior ingredients to their products. To increase shelf-life they may add preservatives and artificial colorings, which may cause adverse health effects.

With a prolonged shelf-life, manufacturers can ship their products farther, keep them there longer, and make them available to more people. While this has its advantages for the food industry, it has had a negative impact on those of us who have come to depend on these processed foods as the mainstay of our diet. When you add attractive packaging and clever advertising to the equation, it becomes possible for food manufacturers to influence our attitudes toward nutrition and our understanding of portion size. Consequently, we have grown accustomed to taking in far more calories than our bodies can use. This overconsumption, stored as fat, has led to one of the most serious health problems facing Americans today: the problem of obesity.

In the United States, obesity is the top nutrition-related disease affecting children. According to a National Health and Nutrition Examination Survey conducted between 1988 and 1994, 11 percent of American children and adolescents were overweight, and some experts today estimate the figure to be closer to one in three.

Even as far back as 1977, health professionals were concerned about childhood obesity and the likelihood that overweight children would become obese adults. Studies showed that the risk increases with each age group. For instance, although fewer than 10% of obese infants become obese adults, the percentage increases to 25% for obese preschoolers and 70% for obese teenagers.

Obesity is not merely a matter of appearance, discomfort, and perhaps some playground teasing. Obese children are at higher risk for cardiovascular disease and high blood pressure. They are more likely to suffer from Type 2 diabetes, a condition once experienced only by adults. This puts them at risk for adult diabetes-related ailments, such as blindness, nerve damage, kidney failure, and cardiovascular disease. Obese children are more likely to have a poor sense of self-esteem. They tend to prefer sedentary activities over sports, which causes them to burn fewer calories and gain even more weight.

A 1994 National Institutes of Health study found that men and women between the ages of 25 and 30 were on average 10 pounds heavier than 25-30 year-olds in 1986. They concluded that Americans are getting fatter for primarily three reasons: our poor eating habits, the poor nutritional quality of the food we eat, and a decrease in the amount of exercise we engage in. They further concluded that early habits do influence obesity later in life; less active children are more likely to become fatter, inactive adults.

Health-care providers weigh and measure children from the time they are born, using these measurements to monitor their overall health. As our children grow older and their visits to the doctor become less frequent, the burden of weight management shifts to us. It becomes our responsibility to ensure that our children are maintaining a healthy weight, that they are eating a nutritionally balanced diet, that they are not eating too much junk food, and that they are exercising regularly. The *Dietary Guidelines for Americans, 5th Edition* recommends that children be physically active for at least 60 minutes a day.

Raising children provides us all with an excellent reason to examine our own eating and fitness habits and to decide which habits we want to pass on to our children and which habits we'd rather they not acquire. The sooner we educate ourselves and set a good example by improving our own eating habits and increasing physical activity, the better off the whole family will be.

> Super-size it? Before saying "yes" think about whether your body really needs more than what is considered a *normal* amount.

Nutrition: What Kids Need

As children grow, their dietary needs change. As long as they continue to eat a variety of nutritious foods and remain active, they should be able to maintain a healthy body weight for the long term.

According to the *Dietary Guidelines for Americans,* children ages 2 to 6, sedentary women and some older adults require about 1600 calories a day. Most children over 6, teen girls, active women, and many sedentary men require about 2200 calories per day. Teen boys and active men need about 2800 calories a day. Make the most of these calories by offering your children whole grains, fruits, and vegetables. The following table provides serving requirements by calorie group and lists examples of serving sizes for each food group.

Daily Serving Requirements

Food Group and Serving Size	Children Ages 2 to 6	Older children, Teen girls	Teen boys
Grains 1 slice of whole-grain bread ½ cup of cooked whole-grain cereal, rice, or pasta	6	9	11
Vegetables 1 cup of raw leafy vegetables ½ cup of other vegetables	3	4	5
Fruits 1 medium apple, orange, pear, peach, or plum; ½ banana ½ cup of chopped fruit	2	3	4
Calcium-rich Foods 1 cup of skim or 1% milk, goat milk, or calcium-enriched soy milk, yogurt, cottage cheese 1 ½ ounces of reduced fat cheese ½ cup of cubed tofu (made with calcium sulfate) ½ cup of cooked broccoli, spinach, turnip greens, chard, kale 3 ounces of canned salmon	3	3	3
Protein-rich Foods 2-3 ounces of cooked lean meat, poultry, or fish ½ cup of cooked dry beans or tofu 2 ½-ounce soyburger 1 egg or egg substitute 2 tablespoons of peanut butter, almond butter, cashew butter, or soy nut butter 1/3 cup of nuts	2	2.5	3

Eating Smart

Switching to a more healthful diet can be a challenge. We live in a society where we are continuously bombarded with advertisements urging us to eat nutrient-poor, highly processed foods. Fast food restaurants offering free toys to children line the streets in almost every city and town. Large signs and billboards beckon us to eat what is quick, convenient, easy, and terribly unhealthy. We are bombarded with television, magazine, and supermarket ads offering us choices that are unhealthful at best, illness-causing at worst. But what can we do?

The American Academy of Pediatrics provides some guidelines for helping children keep healthy and fit. They suggest that parents provide a variety of healthy foods and limit fat intake. Children over the age of two should limit fat intake to less than 30 percent of their total daily calories. Limiting fast foods, which are high in fat and sodium and are generally sold in large portions, is a good place to start. Prepare foods at home as often as you can. Involve children in food selection and preparation. Children are more likely to eat food that they've helped choose and prepare, and cooking will educate them about what's in the food they eat. Offer water instead of fruit juice, juice drinks, or soda. Make sure your children get enough calcium. Encourage them to eat slowly and to truly enjoy the ritual of eating, and make sure they get plenty of sleep.

Children who eat well experience less fatigue, have more energy, and have better concentration. They are more fit for sports and other physical activities, and they have a lower obesity rate.

If you feel that your family diet is not what you'd like it to be, try to incorporate the following suggestions, one at a time, into your daily routine.

Eat a Variety of Fresh Vegetables and Fruits Daily

Fruits and vegetables are essential because they provide carbohydrates, vitamins, minerals, and fiber. They contain calcium, iron, and trace minerals. They are cholesterol- and fat-free and are naturally low in calories. Studies have shown that eating at least five servings of fruits and vegetables a day protects against heart disease and cancer.

Remember that heating and processing foods may cause nutrient loss. To maximize the nutrient value of fruits and vegetables, buy them fresh from local sources whenever possible. Fruits and vegetables that have traveled long and far to reach your kitchen are likely to be less nutritious. Eat fruits and vegetables raw or try cooking them for short periods of time. Choose steaming over boiling to minimize nutrient loss. If you cook them in advance, reheat just before serving rather than keeping them warm for longer periods of time.

If you have a child who does not like to eat vegetables, offer them anyway, at least twice a day. Don't force them on your child, but do encourage them to try at least two bites of each food. Try offering vegetables first, when your child is most hungry. Be positive, firm, and patient, and wait a few minutes before bringing out the rest of the meal. Refrain from bargaining, cajoling, or begging. Sit down with your children and enjoy eating vegetables together. They will soon come to understand that vegetables are an important part of every meal.

> *Tip:*
>
> If your children ask for food while you're cooking dinner, serve a salad or veggie platter to tide them over.

Limit Processed Foods

Whenever a food is processed, it loses some of its nutritional value. Processed foods typically contain added sugar, salt, and/or hydrogenated fats. Most also contain additives, including preservatives, colorings, and flavorings. Read labels carefully. To get the most out of your food, choose unprocessed products as often as possible. Before purchasing a a processed food, ask yourself whether there might be an unprocessed alternative available. In most cases, you will be able to find one. For example, substitute fresh sliced apples for sweetened applesauce and fresh cucumbers for pickles. Instead of buying processed lunch meats, slice up some freshly broiled turkey or chicken.

Remember that unprocessed foods, even some organic varieties, may be less expensive than their processed counterparts. When an item is heavily packaged, the cost of the packaging is passed on to the consumer. To remain competitive some manufacturers are forced to use less costly, nutritionally inferior ingredients in their products. If you'd like to get more nutrition for your money by cutting down on processed foods, consider making some of the following changes.

- Buy five-minute oatmeal instead of one-minute oatmeal. Cooking takes only four minutes longer, and the added nutrition is worth it.
- Buy unprocessed rice instead of instant varieties.
- Buy fresh fruits and vegetables instead of canned. (Keep frozen vegetables on hand for emergencies.)
- Flavor your food with individual herbs and spices rather than relying on prepackaged flavorings. (Read the labels and you'll see why.)
- Make your own salad dressings using quality ingredients such as 100% extra-virgin olive oil, vinegar or lemon juice, soy mayonnaise, or Dijon mustard instead of purchasing ready-made dressings. It takes only minutes more and with just a few ingredients, you can make a wide variety of dressings. Some salad cookbooks contain lists of excellent salad dressing recipes. Try a new one each evening for dinner and conduct a week-long salad dressing taste test with the family.
- Make soups from scratch instead of purchasing canned varieties. Make a large pot and freeze some in smaller containers for future use.
- Check bread labels. The best breads contain at least 2 grams of fiber per slice. They are made up of easy-to-pronounce ingredients— whole-wheat (or other whole-grain) flour, yeast, water, honey, and sea salt. If you find a lot of other ingredients on the label, think twice. Avoid bread that contains bleached flour. (Dioxin, which is a by-product of the bleaching process, may cause cancer, infertility, endometriosis, and birth defects.) Consider baking bread with your

kids once in a while. It's a fun activity, and it's a great way to teach them where their food comes from!

- Purchase unprocessed (preferably organic) meats instead of buying processed lunch meats. If you're not sure what you're buying, read labels or ask the butcher. If you are in the habit of buying processed meats from the deli counter, ask the clerk to provide you with a list of ingredients before purchasing. In place of these meats, use leftovers for sandwiches or choose a vegetarian alternative. If you prepare meat for dinner, prepare a few extra servings to use for lunch in sandwiches or as a main dish.

- Stay away from chips. To get the most out of your potatoes, try them baked, mashed, or pan-fried. To reap the benefits from corn, try a piece of fresh corn-on-the-cob. Check the labels of "healthy" chips carefully before buying. They may not be as healthy as you think. Choose fat-free pretzels, preferably whole-wheat or oat, for added nutritional value.

- Avoid prepackaged desserts. You won't find many nutrients there. Instead, choose healthy treats, such as fresh or dried unsulfured fruits, or try some of our tasty recipes on pages 73-75.

Did you know...

40-60 % of the calories in an average fast-food meal come from fat?

Limit Fats

Our bodies need a limited amount of fat in order to function properly, but not all fats are alike. Generally, non-hydrogenated fats and oils from plant sources such as nuts, seeds, and olives are considered beneficial. Fats derived from animal sources, such as meat and dairy products, should be limited.

Two of the best cooking oils are extra-virgin olive oil and sesame oil. For salads and other cold dishes try extra-virgin olive or walnut oil.

Healthy school-age children and teenagers should derive no more than 30 percent of their total daily calories from fat. Sadly, with our over-reliance on foods like hamburgers, hot dogs, fried chicken, French fries, pizza, chips and processed desserts, many children far exceed this amount.

Eating large quantities of fats affects our bodies in many ways. Here's what *The Family Nutrition Book* has to say about the negative effects of saturated fats and hydrogenated oils:

- They damage and clog arteries.
- They raise the level of LDL (bad) cholesterol and reduce the level of HDL (good) cholesterol in the blood, increasing the risk of heart disease and stroke.
- They inhibit the body's ability to regulate many of its vital functions.
- When we eat fast foods and processed products, we consume a large amount of these damaging fats. By not making healthier choices, we deprive ourselves of the good fats our bodies need.

Some of these concerns may not seem serious for children and teens, but food preferences formed early in life tend to prevail in adulthood. Limiting high-fat foods, especially fried foods, baked goods, meats, and dairy products now, while training the palate to enjoy more wholesome foods, may induce children to make better food choices later on. Also, limiting dietary fat now may help prevent cumulative health problems as we age. If you're concerned about fat intake, consider limiting the following foods.

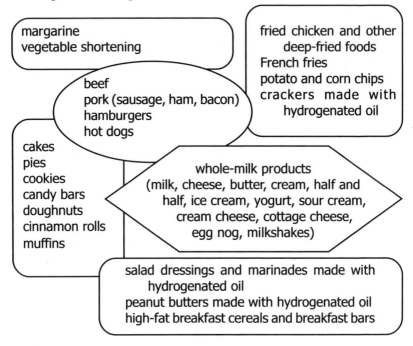

margarine
vegetable shortening

fried chicken and other deep-fried foods
French fries
potato and corn chips
crackers made with hydrogenated oil

beef
pork (sausage, ham, bacon)
hamburgers
hot dogs

cakes
pies
cookies
candy bars
doughnuts
cinnamon rolls
muffins

whole-milk products
(milk, cheese, butter, cream, half and half, ice cream, yogurt, sour cream, cream cheese, cottage cheese, egg nog, milkshakes)

salad dressings and marinades made with hydrogenated oil
peanut butters made with hydrogenated oil
high-fat breakfast cereals and breakfast bars

Limit Sweets

Refined sugar and sugar substitutes do not provide the body with essential nutrients, which is why calories derived from sugar are called "empty calories." Children who consume large amounts of sugary sweets may do so instead of eating nutrient-rich foods such as fruits and vegetables. An overconsumption of sugar, or any food for that matter, can lead to obesity when the body stores it as fat.

In addition to the increased risk of obesity, excess sugar consumption is thought to depress immunity. It has been linked to diabetes and heart disease, and may increase the risk of cancer.

Sugar consumption increases the risk of dental decay. In countries where sugar consumption is low, the incidence of dental cavities is also low, and in countries where sugar consumption is higher, the incidence of dental cavities is higher. According to Linda Peavy and Andrea Pagenkopf, in their book, *Grow Healthy Kids!*, about 95 percent of American children have no cavities at the age of 1. However, by age 2, 5 to 10 percent have some cavities. This increases to 40-55 percent for 3-year-olds and to 75 percent for 5-year-olds. In fact, the average American 5-year-old has 4.6 decayed or filled teeth. As children grow older and they gradually consume more and more sugar, the number of cavities increases.

Studies of the effects of sugar consumption on behavior have produced contradictory results. However, some teachers and parents will attest to the fact that some children appear to be sugar sensitive. Consuming sugary foods in the absence of a balanced diet results in a negative impact on behavior and on a child's ability to concentrate and learn effectively.

If your children are accustomed to eating high-sugar foods and you would like to replace these foods with nutrient-rich choices, there are several steps you can take. The most important first step is to educate the family on the risks of a high-sugar diet and the benefits of a balanced diet. Check your local library or book store for age-appropriate materials for your children. Limit the amount of high-sugar food that is brought into the house. (Don't go food shopping on an empty stomach, and don't give in to pleas for junk food that your children have seen advertised on television.) Make wise dessert choices for the entire family.

Come up with a family plan for reducing sugar consumption. If your children are old enough, involve them in the decision-making part of the plan. Get the whole family involved. Elicit help with food preparation. Encourage your children to pack their own lunches or to help you pack them. Find out what nutritious foods they like best and make sure they're readily available. To wean them from lunchtime desserts, try fresh fruit or a non-food treat such as stickers for younger children.

Try some of the following strategies if you'd like to reduce your family's consumption of sweets.

- Limit products that are high in sugar, including corn syrup, corn sweetener, fructose, fruit juice concentrate, granular fruit sugar, sucrose, lactose, isomol, malitol, mannitol, sorbitol, maltose, xylitol, malt, honey, maple sugar, maple syrup, molasses, and rice syrup.
- Substitute a very small amount of honey, maple syrup, molasses, applesauce, or brown rice syrup for refined sugar. You can use much less of these to achieve the same sweetness.
- Read product labels, keeping in mind that ingredients are listed in order of greatest to least amount. Remember, too, that many manufacturers include more than one sugar ingredient in a given product so that sugar will not appear as the first or second ingredient on the list.
- Serve fruit for dessert and snacks instead of sugary sweets.
- When baking, reduce the amount of sugar by one-half or one-third. Freeze extras for special occasions.
- Eliminate soft drinks, sports drinks, and fruit drinks, which are nothing more than cleverly marketed sugar water.

Limit Sodium

Processed foods are generally high in sodium, which increases the risk of high blood pressure and stroke. Children who eat a limited amount of sodium are less likely to crave heavily salted foods later in life when the incidence of high blood pressure and stroke is much greater.

If you are concerned about the amount of salt (sodium chloride) your children are consuming, put away the salt shaker and select foods that are labeled low- or reduced-sodium. Limit salty foods such as chips, crackers, pretzels, salted nuts, soy sauce, pickles, some cereals, cheese, and processed lunch meats. Read labels carefully, especially when choosing processed products.

Eat a Variety of High-fiber Foods

The benefits of a fiber-rich diet are many. Fiber helps reduce the risk of diabetes, constipation, and some types of cancer; and it can lower blood cholesterol. People who eat high-fiber foods are less likely to overeat for two reasons: fiber stays in the stomach longer, making us feel full faster and longer; and digesting it requires more chewing, which satisfies the muscles around the mouth and jaw.

It is easy to see that your children get enough fiber in their diet by serving them whole grains, vegetables, and fruits. Here are a few suggestions for adding fiber to their diet. Make changes gradually, and be sure to increase fluid intake as you increase the intake of fiber.

- Serve whole, unpeeled fruits, rather than fruit juices.
- Buy dried fruits.
- Choose whole-grain bread, flour, rice, pasta, cereal, and other similar products in place of refined white varieties.
- Serve whole-grain cereals instead of high-sugar varieties.
- Provide at least 2-3 servings of dark green, red, and orange vegetables daily.
- Choose beans, nuts, and whole grains for protein instead of meat, eggs, and dairy products.

If your family isn't accustomed to eating fiber-rich foods, introduce them one at a time. Start by adding a small amount of brown rice to your white rice, and gradually increase the percentage of brown rice each time you make it. Do the same when making pasta. When you buy bread, bagels, tortillas, English muffins, and pocket bread, gradually switch to whole-grain varieties. Replace low-fiber/high-sugar breakfast cereals with more wholesome varieties. Read labels carefully; product names and health claims can be deceiving.

Did you know...

it takes three medium-size oranges to make just one cup of juice? Keep in mind that children can fill up easily when offered fruit juice before or during meals.

Emphasize Plant-based Foods

According to the U.S. Dietary Guidelines, children between the ages of one and six need only 5 ounces of protein daily. This increases to 6 ounces for older children and 7 ounces for active teen boys. The protein in our diet can be derived from a broad range of sources, but most of us rely too heavily on meat-based sources of protein.

With the typical American diet centering around meat, most of us eat far more protein than we actually need, which puts us at greater risk for chronic diseases. The average American consumes two to three times the recommended amount of protein. Since much of this protein comes from animal sources and is high in saturated fat, the American Heart Association recommends cutting down on the amount of food derived from animals.

Still there are other reasons to consume fewer animal-based foods. First, conventional farms, including those growing animal feed, rely heavily on pesticides, herbicides, and chemical fertilizers. These products are then eaten by the animals and stored in their fat. When we consume animal products that are high in fat, we consume the chemical compounds stored there. These stay with us for a long time, continuing to accumulate as we age.

Secondly, animals are routinely treated with hormones to promote rapid growth and with antibiotics to prevent disease. When we eat their meat, the residues can enter our bodies where they are stored in our fat. In addition, processed meats contain additives such as nitrites and nitrates, which have been linked to several types of cancer.

If you are concerned about these health issues, and you would like to reduce the amount of meat you eat, try making some of the following changes.

- Serve smaller portions of protein.
- Plan meals around grains, using protein as an ingredient instead of the focal point.
- Choose a vegetarian option for 1-2 meals daily.
- Cut out processed meats such as deli lunch meats and hot dogs. (Read prepackaged meat labels to see why.)
- Switch to organic meat (or meatless) products.
- Serve beef no more than once a week, and choose leaner cuts, such as top round, eye of round, round tip, or bottom round.
- Remove the skin from poultry before cooking and choose white meat over dark meat.
- Choose free-range products whenever possible.
- Educate your family on the benefits of a plant-based diet. Come up with a family plan for eating less animal-based food.

As a family, talk about the other consequences that result from a society dependent on a meat-based diet. In particular, you may want to discuss the inhumane treatment of animals raised for food, the contamination of our soil, and the contamination and depletion of our water supply. Be sure to mention that harmful chemicals used on crops eaten by animals can accumulate in our bodies. Discuss the inefficiency of using land for meat production compared to growing plants for human consumption, mentioning that a farmer can grow 20,000 pounds of potatoes on one acre of land, but if he chooses to plant cattle feed instead, he will produce enough for only 165 pounds of beef. Don't forget to discuss the global effects as well: world hunger, deforestation, and loss of species.

Search for vegetarian cookbooks and vegetarian how-to books at your local library or bookstore, at flea markets and at yard sales. In particular, look for books with full-color photographs of nutritious, well-presented food. Have your family pick out the recipes that look appealing and enlist their help in buying groceries and preparing meals. Consider viewing the one-hour video *Diet for a New America* by John Robbins, available at some libraries. It can serve as a springboard for passionate, in-depth discussions.

If your family is resistant, start by introducing just one vegetarian meal a week. Choose recipes that are hearty and filling to start. After a few weeks, prepare two vegetarian meals a week, gradually increasing the number over time. When you serve meat, de-emphasize it. Try making stir-frys, stews, soups, pasta dishes, and salads—all with fresh vegetables. Gradually reduce the amount of meat in the dish, or replace the meat with plant-based proteins such as tofu, lentils or kidney beans, and whole grains.

Be careful not to go overboard on eggs and dairy products. Do not replace high-fat meat with high-fat milk. Instead, introduce interesting grains and legumes. Try meat substitutes such as tofu hot dogs, and veggie burgers. Try textured vegetable protein instead of ground beef. Get your family hooked on tofu by preparing it in a variety of ways.

Reducing our reliance on animal-based proteins is a family affair. Remember, as parents we must set a good example. We must change our own habits of excessive protein consumption if we are going to ask our children to change theirs. By reducing the amount of animal food we consume as a family, we teach our children respect for themselves, for others, for our animals, and for our planet.

Drink Plenty of Water

Our bodies need a constant supply of water for optimal performance. A shortage of water can lead to dehydration, constipation, fatigue, and an inability to concentrate well. Water can be derived not only from the liquids we drink, but also from food sources such as soups, sauces, vegetables, and fruits. Water can also be found in sodas, fruit and sports drinks, and other high-sugar, high (empty) calorie beverages, which tend to fill children up without providing them with any essential nutrients. Serving water instead of these sweet alternatives will leave room for other nutrient-rich foods.

Water is naturally calorie-free. It contains no sugar, artificial sweeteners, preservatives or colorings. It contains no caffeine, citric acid, or phosphoric acid, which can inhibit the absorption of calcium. *The Family Nutrition Book* estimates that a 12-ounce cola can rob the body of 100 milligrams of calcium.

Encourage your children to make water their drink of choice. Pack water in their lunchboxes instead of sodas or sweetened fruit drinks. Order water at restaurants. Teach your children to enjoy the taste of water now so that they will enjoy drinking it for the rest of their lives.

Avoid Overeating

Eating too much of anything, be it fat, carbohydrate, or protein, can lead to obesity and its associated health risks. Creating meals that emphasize fruits, vegetables, whole grains, and just a small amount of protein will provide the best balance for good health and weight control.

Buy Certified Organic and Locally Grown Produce

Organic products are becoming increasingly more available to the general public. Twenty years ago, natural food stores were few and far between, but times are changing fast. Even large corporations have begun to see that the demand for organic foods is on the rise, and they don't want to miss out. This is made evident by the large number of natural food stores popping up across the country and the number of traditional supermarkets now offering organic choices.

Most U.S. cities and many towns now have at least one store where shoppers can find organic products, and major cities have many more. Catalogue companies and e-commerce businesses, too, have joined the ranks of companies offering organic products to ready consumers.

Check your local telephone directory, chamber of commerce, and the Internet to find out what options are available to you. Check also with friends and neighbors for ideas on where to buy organic foods.

Whatever your situation, eating organic foods will certainly...

- minimize your intake of potentially harmful chemicals
- protect water quality by keeping harmful chemicals out of the water supply
- prevent soil erosion
- protect wildlife
- support sustainable farming practices
- support farmers who are committed to producing high-quality food and protecting the environment
- support farmers who promote biodiversity by growing greater varieties of fruits, vegetables, and grains, instead of relying heavily on single high-market demand varieties
- allow you to enjoy great taste and full flavor

If you can't find organic produce in your area, speak to the manager at your favorite supermarket and request that they start an organic produce section there. Talk to your friends and have them express an interest as well. You never know what might happen! If the supermarket does satisfy your request, increase the program's likelihood of success by recommending it to all your friends and acquaintances. If organic products sell well, the supermarket will be eager to expand their offerings and carry a greater selection of organic foods.

If you live in an area where food is grown, consider shopping at farmer's markets or join a CSA (Community Supported Agriculture) program. You may be able to receive a weekly share of seasonal organic farm-fresh produce straight from the farm at a great price.

Pesticide residues in the food we eat vary greatly from product to product. The effects of these residues on each of us is determined not only by the toxicity of the chemical, but also by our body weight and the amount of the chemical we consume. Pesticide residues pose a greater health risk to children than to adults because children have a low body weight and tend to rely more heavily on certain foods, such as dairy and apple products. To minimize the effects of pesticides, buy organic varieties of the foods your children eat most frequently and make sure that your family eats a wide variety of foods.

Another way to reduce pesticide intake is to eat foods with a low toxicity index (TI). The higher the TI, the higher the pesticide residue. The Consumers Union, a nonprofit publisher of *Consumer Reports* and the Environmental Working Group have recently published reports on the pesticide residues found on domestically-grown and imported fruits and vegetables. Their combined findings indicated the following:

The 12 most contaminated fruits and vegetables

apples	peaches
bell peppers	pears
celery	potatoes
cherries	raspberries
grapes	spinach
nectarines	strawberries

The 12 least contaminated fruits and vegetables

asparagus	kiwi
avocados	mangos
bananas	onions
broccoli	papayas
cauliflower	pineapples
corn	peas

Keep in mind that updated reports are released from time to time, so it is important to remain informed. For the latest information and a printer friendly wallet guide, visit http://www.foodnews.org/walletguide.php.

The Consumer's Union and the Environmental Working Group have not analyzed foods such as dairy products for other substances like hormones and antibiotics, which are routinely given to dairy cows. While the presence of hormones, antibiotics, and pesticide residues in dairy products remains controversial, you may want to consider buying organic dairy products if your children consume milk, cheese, yogurt, butter, and other dairy products regularly.

If you have the time, the space, and the right climate, consider planting your own organic garden. Kids are more likely to eat something they've grown themselves, and caring for a garden increases their awareness of where their food comes from. Start a compost pile of grass, plant trimmings, and fallen leaves. From your kitchen add a regular supply of fruit and vegetable trimmings, egg shells, and coffee grounds. Check your local library, bookstore, or the Internet for more information on composting.

Transitioning to a Smart Lunch

Making the transition to a smart lunch involves many aspects of our lives, such as educating the family and stocking the kitchen with healthy lunch choices. To do this effectively, it is necessary to read food labels carefully and to think critically about what foods to purchase. Start now. The sooner you begin, the more receptive your children will be.

Educating Your Family

Education is the first step in the transition to a smart lunch. Talk to your children about why your family is making these changes. Provide them with age-appropriate information about the negative impact of a wasteful, unhealthy lunch. Below is a list of suggestions that will help build communication and foster understanding.

- Teach children about recycling at home. Encourage them to help separate the recyclables from the non-recyclables.
- When you choose not to buy an excessively packaged item, point it out to your children and ask if they can think of some earth-friendly packaging alternatives.
- If possible, take a trip to your local landfill or recycling facility.
- Find books on nutrition and waste reduction at your local library or bookstore. Read them together and discuss how these issues relate to your lives.
- Discuss where foods come from and how much processing occurs before they get to your table. Compare, for example, a baked potato and a bag of potato chips.
- Together, make a poster of *growing foods* by drawing pictures or cutting them from magazines and supermarket ads. (Make a second poster with all of the other foods you see advertised.)

- Search your local, preferably used, bookstore for some good health-oriented cookbooks, including some with large color photographs that you can share with your children. Read them together, look at the photographs, and ask your children to show you which recipes they find most appealing. Make a shopping list together, buy the necessary ingredients, and give the recipes a try.
- Teach older children how to read nutrition labels on food packages. Together, compare products at the supermarket and ask your children to help you make the most nutritionally-sound choices based on the fat, fiber, sugar, and sodium content. Look at ingredient lists and discuss what each ingredient is and what it does (or doesn't do) for the body.
- When eating out, talk about which restaurants are most likely to offer nutritious choices. Make this one of the main criterion for choosing a restaurant.
- Urge your children to order healthy meals from the regular menu instead of relying solely on children's menus, which tend to offer high-fat (fried), high sodium, fiberless choices.

Smart Shopping

Below is a list of practical suggestions for buying better quality food for your family. Start by incorporating just one or two. Once you have celebrated a success or two, make more changes, starting with the ones that are easiest for your family to make.

- Shop in stores that carry the most nutritious foods.
- Buy local organic produce at farmer's markets if you can find them in your area.
- Read labels (see pages 33-44). Are you buying a particular product out of habit? Is there a more healthful choice such as a different brand or an unprocessed alternative?

- Buy nutritious foods in bulk. (Read nutrition labels carefully before buying.)
- Buy foods that remember where they come from. For example, choose corn-on-the-cob over corn chips. Choose fresh fruit instead of fruit bars or fruit-flavored roll-ups.
- Buy organic products whenever you can. Buy seasonal produce. Buy non-perishable products in quantity when they are on sale.
- Don't let your children convince you to make unhealthy purchases at the store. It's okay to say "no" when they ask for a candy bar at the checkout stand.
- Don't let your children convince you to purchase unhealthy foods they've seen advertised on TV. Keep in mind that children often make food choices based solely on attractive packaging. (Younger children may not even know what's inside the package!) Talk with them about how to make wise choices, provide them with a healthy snack before going to the grocery store, and stand firm.
- If your children ask for something that you do not want to buy, but you would like to buy them a treat, provide nutritious choices instead, and let them choose from among them. If, for example, your child asks for a fruit roll-up, tell her that she can pick out a basket of berries. Let her decide which type of berry to buy.
- If your children are following you through the store begging for one item after the next, tell them, "If it's not on the list, we're not buying it," and stand firm. If they are old enough, give them an item on the list to find. Divert their attention by engaging them in food selection.
- Keep a shopping list in the kitchen to keep track of what you need to buy. When you see that you are running low on a particular item, make a quick note. Take the list shopping with you so you will remember to pick up the nutritious foods that keep your kitchen well supplied.
- To encourage participation from everyone in the family, try having a family "cupboard cleaning party." Throw out (or donate) all of the food that you have deemed unhealthy. Replace these foods with more nutritionally acceptable choices.

Stocking your Kitchen with Smart Choices

The following is a list of changes you can make when restocking your kitchen with wholesome foods. As a family, decide which changes you can make easily and start with those. Try to find organic products whenever possible.

- Replace refined grains with their whole-grain counterparts. Try a variety of grains, such as whole wheat, rye, oats, oat bran, amaranth, buckwheat, quinoa, bulghar, wheat germ, brown rice, and barley.
- Update your cereal supply with healthier whole-grain, low sodium varieties that contain minimal sugar, no hydrogenated oils, and no preservatives.
- Substitute refined white pasta with healthier, organic varieties, such as whole wheat, amaranth, and pastas colored with vegetable juices.
- Replace canned fruit with unsulphured bulk dried fruit such as apples, peaches, pears, raisins, prunes, apricots, cranberries, pineapple, mango, and papaya.
- Buy a variety of nuts and seeds in bulk. Try almonds, walnuts, pecans, cashews, sesame seeds, flax seeds, sunflower seeds, and pumpkin seeds.
- Replace meat-based products with tofu and other soy products, such as tofu hot dogs, baked tofu, firm tofu for stir-frys, and "ground tofu" instead of ground beef for tacos and sloppy joes.
- Make sure you have honey, 100% maple syrup, and molasses on hand as sweeteners. You can use much less of these to attain the same sweetness as refined sugar.
- Purchase extra-virgin olive oil and other fruit and nut oils instead of vegetable oils.
- Avoid solvent-extracted oils which can contain harmful residual chemicals. If your oil does not say how it was extracted, assume that solvents were used.

- Avoid products that contain hydrogenated oils, which are commonly found in crackers, cookies, and other processed foods.
- Look for organic alternatives to the condiments normally found in your refrigerator. They may be cheaper than name brands and contain fewer or no additives. For example, replace high-fat mayonnaise or chemical-laden fat-free mayonnaise with a soy-based mayonnaise. Buy organic ketchup and mustard.
- Purchase quality sea salt, tamari, and soy sauce instead of table salt. Sea salt contains all the trace elements that our bodies require without chemical manipulation.
- Stock up on bulk dried legumes such as lentils, kidney beans, and pinto beans.
- Buy bulk almond butter and peanut butter instead of national brands that may contain added sugar, salt and hydrogenated oil. (Refrigerate immediately to prevent natural separation from occurring.)

Reading Food Labels

Processed foods are attractively packaged. They are given appealing names that do not always reflect the healthfulness of the food inside. It is, therefore, necessary to read labels routinely to find out whether a particular product is, indeed, as wholesome as the manufacturer claims. Here are a few tips for reading product labels:

- Remember that ingredients are listed in the order of quantity present. The first few ingredients on the list are there in the greatest quantity.
- Check to make sure that the first few ingredients are the ones you would hope to find in this type of product. For example, on a grape juice label you expect to see grape juice listed first. If, instead, you saw corn syrup, high fructose corn syrup, fruit pectin and then grape juice concentrate, you would know that this product is far less nutritious than a product made of 100% grape juice.
- Beware of misleading food groupings that make it look like an undesirable ingredient is present in lesser quantities. For instance, breakfast cereal manufacturers often group flour ingredients together so that sugar will not appear as the first ingredient. A label of this type might list the first two ingredients as flour (corn, wheat, and oat), and then sugar. If the flours had not been grouped together, sugar would have been listed as the first ingredient.

- Beware of products that contain multiple sweeteners. A product may contain, for example, sugar, high fructose corn syrup, corn syrup, and dextrose. Although sugar does not appear first on the list, when added together, the total sugar is present in the greatest quantity.
- When evaluating foods, think twice about purchasing products with the following red flag warnings on the label.

  ☹ The ingredients list seems long compared to what you'd expect to find in a particular product.

  ☹ The ingredients are unrecognizable and hard to pronounce.

  ☹ The product contains FD&C artificial colorings.

  ☹ The product contains hydrogenated or partially-hydrogenated oil.

  ☹ One of the first few ingredients listed is sugar (or other sweeteners such as high fructose corn syrup, corn sweetener, fructose, fruit juice concentrate, granular fruit sugar, sucrose, lactose, isomol, malitol, mannitol, sorbitol, maltose, xylitol, malt, honey, maple sugar, maple syrup, molasses, or rice syrup).

  ☹ The product contains the artificial sweeteners aspartame or saccharin.

  ☹ The product contains modified food starch, which is often used as an inexpensive filler.

  ☹ The product contains a large amount of salt. The human body needs no more than ¼ teaspoon of salt daily. Try to limit intake to 2,400 mg (1 teaspoon) of total sodium daily.

Beware...

Some foods may not be as healthy as they first seem. Many processed fruit- and vegetable-enhanced products may contain nothing more than food coloring.

A Closer Look at Some Popular Lunch Items

Below is a list of ingredients found in some common lunch foods. For each product, we have included at least one popular choice and at least one healthier alternative. Look at the ingredients list and notice how they differ in length. If you want to get an even better idea of what these products contain, circle the ingredients that you consider okay, and cross out the ones you'd rather not serve to your children.

Bread

National-Brand White Bread

Ingredients: Enriched wheat flour, B vitamins, water, high fructose corn syrup, contains 2% or less of soybean oil, yeast, salt, soy flour, calcium sulfate, dough conditioners (sodium stearoyl, lactylate, calcium iodate, calcium dioxide), dicalcium phosphate, diammonium phosphate, monocalcium phosphate, monoglycerides, ammonium sulfate, enzymes, calcium propionate, soy fiber, guar gum, cellulose gum

National-Brand Whole-Wheat Bread

> **Ingredients:** Whole wheat flour, water, high fructose corn syrup, wheat gluten, cracked wheat, honey, partially hydrogenated soybean oil, salt, yeast, molasses, wheat bran, raisin juice concentrate, sodium stearoyl lactylate, grain vinegar, calcium sulfate, monoglycerides, sodium propionate, soy lecithin

Now contrast these products with the ingredients you would find in organic or homemade whole-wheat bread, which is made from higher quality ingredients and contains no additives.

Home-Made Whole-Wheat Bread

> **Ingredients:** Organic whole-wheat flour, water, honey, yeast, and sea salt

This type of bread does not necessarily have to come from your own kitchen. Some quality bakeries and natural food stores carry bread with these same ingredients. See if you can find them in your community.

Yogurt

Yogurt quality varies considerably. Most yogurts contain large amounts of added sweeteners and sweetened fruit. Some even come packaged with sugary toppings of cookie crumbs, chocolate candy pieces, or granola. Quality yogurt is valuable not only for its calcium content, but also for its active cultures, so make sure your yogurt contains them.

This first example is a fruit flavored product. Notice that, since it contains no fruit whatsoever, we cannot tell from the label what flavor it is. Notice, too, that it contains no beneficial yogurt cultures.

National-Brand Yogurt

Ingredients: Cultured pasteurized grade A milk, sugar, nonfat milk, high fructose corn syrup, modified corn starch, kosher gelatin, tricalcium phosphate, natural and artificial flavor, potassium sorbate, carrageenan, colored with carmine, Blue #1

Healthier Yogurt

Ingredients: Cultured pasteurized organic lowfat milk, naturally milled organic sugar, organic non-fat dried milk, organic natural vanilla, pectin. Made with multiple organisms. Live active cultures: S. Thermophilus, L. Bulgaricus, L. Acidophilus, B. Bifidum L. Casei, L. Reuteri

The following organic variety of plain yogurt contains no gelatin or added sweeteners. Instead it contains live yogurt cultures that are good for the digestive tract. Let your children add their own fresh fruit. It's more nutritious, it tastes better, and it's more fun.

Healthiest Yogurt

Ingredients: Certified organic skim milk, organic skim milk powder, S. Thermophilus, L. Bulgaricus, L. Acidophilus, B. Bifidum Cultures

Meats

Meat manufacturers must preserve their products to prevent the growth of unwanted bacteria. They can do this by freezing their products or by adding chemical preservatives and sodium-based curing agents. Here are two examples of deli meats that contain chemical preservatives:

Deli Ham

Ingredients: Ham, water, contains less than 2% of sugar, Sodium lactate, Sodium phosphate, Sodium erythrobate (made from sugar), Sodium diacetate, Sodium nitrate

Deli Turkey

Ingredients: White turkey, turkey broth, corn syrup, Potassium lactate, modified food starch, contains 2% or less of celery juice, salt, Sodium phosphate, Sodium diacetate, flavorings

Compare this to a product that has been frozen, thawed, and cooked at home with seasonings. Notice that no fillers, sweeteners, or chemical preservatives have been added.

Home-Broiled Chicken

Ingredients: Chicken, seasonings

Peanut Butter

Peanut butter is another product that may contain unnecessary additives. Compare the two peanut butter products below.

National-Brand Peanut Butter

> **Ingredients:** Roasted peanuts, sugar, partially hydrogenated vegetable oils (rape seed, cottonseed, and soybean), salt

Healthier Peanut Butter

> **Ingredients:** Peanuts

If you buy the first product, you add unnecessary sugar, hydrogenated oils and salt to your family's diet. However, the second product contains exactly what you would hope to find in peanut butter: peanuts. If you are worried that your children won't like natural peanut butter, try starting with one that contains salt since this will be the most noticeable missing ingredient. Later make the switch to the salt-free variety. Once they begin to taste peanuts instead of sugar, salt, and oil, they will truly appreciate the difference.

ToasterTarts, Fruit Bars, and Homemade Oatmeal Bars

Other products that may be particularly deceptive are the ubiquitous so-called "health bars," also known as fruit bars, breakfast bars, granola bars, energy bars, and power bars. Look closely at these products before purchasing. They may be nothing more than cleverly packaged toaster tarts or candy bars. Don't be fooled into seeing these foods as a viable substitute for fruit. If your child has eaten the requisite fruit and vegetables at meal time and still has room, consider choosing one of the last two alternatives.

Strawberry-Flavored Toaster Tarts (unfrosted)

Filling: Corn syrup, dextrose, high fructose corn syrup, cracker meal, modified wheat starch, partially hydrogenated soybean oil, dried strawberries, dried apples, citric acid, sugar, pectin, xanthan gum, water, soy lecithin, red #40 **Crust:** enriched wheat flour, partially hydrogenated soybean oil, corn syrup, sugar, dextrose, salt, high fructose corn syrup, leavening (baking soda, sodium acid pyrophosphate, monocalcium phosphate, calcium sulfate), niacinamide, reduced iron, vitamin A palmitate, pyridoxine hydrochloride (vitamin B6), riboflavin (vitamin B2), thiamin hydrochloride (vitamin B1), and folic acid

Strawberry-Flavored Fruit Bars

Filling: sugar, high fructose corn syrup, corn syrup, strawberry puree, modified food starch, apple powder, apple puree, dextrose, water, glycerin, citric acid, pectin, sodium citrate, caramel color, salt, malic acid, sodium benzoate (preservative), natural flavors, xanthan gum, red #40, sulfur dioxide (color retention). **Crust:** Enriched flour, oatmeal, sugar, high fructose corn syrup, partially hydrogenated soybean oil, (may also contain cottonseed oil), honey, dextrose, tricalcium phosphate (a source of calcium). Nonfat dry milk, soy lecithin (an emulsifier), salt, sodium bicarbonate, artificial flavor, niacinamide, vitamin A palmitate, beta carotene (for color), pyridoxine hydrochloride (vitamin B6), riboflavin (vitamin B2), thiamin mononitrate, folic acid

Healthier Granola Bars

Ingredients: Organic rolled oats, organic honey, brown rice, expeller pressed canola oil, nonfat dry milk, pure barley malt, almonds, natural vanilla, and hazelnut flavors

If you have time to bake, or you have a quality bakery in your area, choose this last alternative. They're delicious, low-waste, and fun to make as a family cooking project (see page 74).

Homemade Oatmeal Bars

> **Ingredients:** Organic oats, organic whole-wheat flour, oil, honey, eggs, water, pure vanilla extract, cinnamon, salt, and baking soda

Drinks

Next time you're out buying food, take a few moments to compare drink labels. You may want to compare the ingredients on the following products: cola, orange flavored drink, "natural" pouch drinks, juice boxes, and water. As you're looking at these labels, make a mental note of what benefits your child derives from each one.

Commonly Used Food Additives

Because commonly used ingredients may be unfamiliar or difficult to pronounce, understanding food labels may take some work. Here's a description of some additives you're likely to encounter.

   Preservatives and curing agents are added to prevent spoilage by slowing down or preventing the growth of bacteria, molds, and yeasts. Some examples include potassium benzoate, sorbic acid (potassium sorbate), sodium nitrate, sodium nitrite, sodium metabisulfite, sodium erythrobate, sodium ascorbate, calcium propionate, sodium propionate, vinegar (acetic acid), sodium diacetate, sodium benzoate, BHA, and BHT.

Stabilizers and thickeners like algin, xanthan gum, and modified food starch, are added to preserve food texture.

Emulsifiers prevent the separation of liquids and solids. Monoglycerides, diglycerides, and egg yolk are commonly used.

Sequestrants prevent trace metals in food from reacting with other ingredients and causing undesirable flavors. EDTA (ethylenediamine tetra acetic acid) is one of the most commonly used.

Flavorings and flavor enhancers are used in an effort to improve the taste of otherwise flavorless foods. MSG (monosodium glutamate), disodium inosinate, and disodium guanylate are some examples.

Colorings, such as annatto extract, caramel coloring, and sulfur dioxide, are added to enhance or preserve color.

Bleaching agents are used to whiten foods and to oxidize wheat flour. These include oxides of nitrogen, chlorine, chlorine dioxide, and benzoyl peroxide.

Acids, alkalies, and buffers, such as citric acid (acid), sodium citrate (buffer), sodium bicarbonate (alkali), and sodium aluminum phosphate (acid), improve flavor and delay spoilage.

Sweeteners come in many different forms, including sugar, corn syrup, corn sweetener, fructose, fruit juice concentrate, granular fruit sugar, sucrose, lactose, isomol, malitol, mannitol, sorbitol, maltose, xylitol, malt, honey, maple sugar, maple syrup, molasses, and rice syrup. The two most widely known **non-nutritive sweeteners** are saccharin and aspartame.

Leavening agents are used for making foods rise. The most commonly used leavenings are yeast, egg whites, baking soda, and baking powder.

Dough conditioners and oxidizing agents prevent food from sticking to machinery and enhance the texture and volume of breads. These include calcium peroxide, potassium bromate, calcium bromate, calcium iodate, calcium stearoly-2-lactylate.

Nutritional additives are those that are added to foods because they are believed to have nutritive benefits. Included in this category are vitamins and minerals. These are most often added back into food to replace the naturally occurring nutrients that have been removed during processing.

Food manufacturers rely heavily on additives to keep costs down and to maintain control over the manufacturing process. By adding substances that prevent dough from sticking to equipment, for example, a large-scale bakery can avoid costly production delays. By adding preservatives they can increase the shelf-life of their products, making it possible for them to be shipped over greater distances and kept on shelves for a longer period of time. Fillers are used because they are less expensive than higher quality ingredients.

While using additives allows manufacturers to maximize profits, it does not necessarily benefit the consumer who is left with a less nutritious product. Read labels carefully and remember that ingredients do change. The national brand products that your parents served you as a child may be quite different from those products bearing the same name today.

> According to the American Academy of Pediatrics, many children will not accept a new food until it has been offered at least ten times.

Strategies for Transitioning the Picky Eater

As some of us know all too well, many children resist change, especially where food is concerned. If you have a picky eater in your family, transitioning to a smart lunch may take some creativity, but don't despair. Be patient, be enthusiastic, and try some of these picky eater strategies.

➜ **Prepare your child.** Talk with your child about nutrition and the importance of developing a healthy body. Together, come up with a family plan, including a list of steps the family can take to transition to a healthier diet. Post the list in a place where everyone can see it.

➜ **Think positively and set a good example.** Believe in your family's success. Participate enthusiastically yourself and your children will likely join in.

➔ **Involve your child.** Children of all ages can help with menu planning, shopping, and meal preparation. When they contribute to the meal in some way, they are more likely to enjoy eating it.

➔ **Introduce a wide variety of foods.** Offer a variety of vegetables, fruits, whole grains, and legumes. Offer a few teaspoons of each at every dinner. Even if your child eats only two bites, she will understand that these are the foods that make up a healthy diet. When she starts wanting more than two bites, expand your offerings to include more foods. As your child grows, increase serving sizes.

➔ **Experiment with old favorites.** Offer a new food with a familiar one. Applaud adventurous eating.

➔ **Offer the same food prepared in different ways.** Offer foods alone and prepared in combination with other ingredients. Cut foods in different ways. Try carrot sticks one day and carrot coins another.

➔ **Don't give up.** According to the American Academy of Pediatrics, many children will not accept a new food until it has been offered at least ten times. Continue to offer new foods until your child considers them familiar.

➔ **Introduce foods one bite or several bites at a time.** Keep portions small. Some children become overwhelmed by large quantities of food on their plate. Others feel that they have acheived success when they have finished the small amount of food provided.

➔ **Serve vegetables and new foods as an appetizer.** If vegetables and new foods are served last or with other foods, children can easily fill themselves up and leave the vegetables behind. Begin dinner, for example, with two green beans and two carrots or a green salad as a starter. When everyone has finished, serve the rest of the meal. Serve fruits with the meal or save them for dessert.

➔ **Institute the "two-bite" rule by requiring children to eat two bites of each item on their plate.** Explain to your children that our tastes change as we grow up. The foods we didn't like last month or last week may taste great now because we've acquired a taste for them. Explain, too, that trying new foods helps build stronger, healthier bodies by developing our palates and allowing us to enjoy a greater variety of foods. Remember that children's food preferences change frequently. What they don't like on Wednesday might be a great hit on Friday or vice versa.

➡ **Consider the possible unspoken meanings of "I don't like it."** "I don't like it" might really mean "I'd rather have a piece of chocolate cake" or "I'm not in the mood for that right now." Insist on the two-bite rule.

➡ **Don't become a short-order cook.** Prepare only one meal for the entire family. At first your child may refuse to eat dinner. Remain calm, stand firm, and ignore tantrums. Your child will not die of hunger from skipping a meal, but will likely come to the next meal with a healthy appetite and a willingness to eat what is served. Allow each family member to plan one nutritionally-balanced dinner a week. Doing so will ensure that everyone has at least one dinner to look forward to.

➡ **Don't make a big deal when your child rejects a food.** Stay cool and reaffirm the boundaries you have established by insisting that your child eat two bites before leaving the table. Don't let your child engage you in a power struggle.

➡ **Give your child a choice.** Give your child some choices within the boundaries you establish. For example, instead of asking, "What do you want for lunch?" ask "Would you like a chicken sandwich or a quesadilla?"

➡ **Do not completely forbid certain foods.** Forbidden foods can quickly become the foods of greatest desire. At school, for example, children are more likely to trade for foods that are not allowed at home. Allow your children to choose a special food from time to time and let them eat it guilt free. Teach your children the difference between everyday foods and occasional foods. In time, they will start making healthy choices on their own.

➡ **Encourage children to bring home their lunch leftovers.** Looking at leftover lunches is a great way to get information about your children's lunch preferences. Find out why certain foods have come back uneaten. Did your child not like it? Was she not hungry enough to eat everything in the lunchbox? Was there a birthday celebration at school that day? Did she share someone else's lunch instead? Maintain a dialogue without criticizing. Consider making a list of foods that your child likes to eat for lunch and update it regularly with input from your child. You may find that she prefers romaine lettuce to red leaf lettuce. By making this simple change, she might start eating salads more regularly. Providing a dip for carrot and celery sticks might make eating them more fun.

➔ **Use the Star Incentive Chart (see Appendix 2).** If your child is resisting the change to a waste-free lunch program, try using the Star Incentive Program described in Appendix 2. Younger children may respond well to stickers, especially if they can help pick them out.

➔ **Use the HealthPoint System (see Appendix 3).** If your child is resisting the change to a healthier diet, try using the HealthPoint System. Allow your child to take one point for each healthy food eaten, four points for each day without junk food, and four points for each day that he exercises. When your child receives a certain agreed-upon number of points by the end of the week, do something special together.

➔ **Avoid food rewards.** Neither dessert nor candy should be used as a punishment or enticement. Rather, you must establish and enforce rules for when and how many treats will be consumed.

Becoming Nutritionally Savvy

Healthy eating does not have to be overt. Try some of these covert ways of improving nutrition by adding extras to your children's food.

- Add finely chopped vegetables and herbs to chicken, tuna, scrambled eggs, omelets, and salmon salad.
- Add parsley and other herbs whenever you can.
- Instead of discarding the water left over from steamed vegetables, use it to cook rice and other grains. After you have steamed your vegetables, pour the liquid into an airtight container and store it in the freezer. When you're ready to cook your grains, defrost and use.
- Add sesame seeds, sunflower seeds, or flax seeds to vegetables, casseroles, pastas, and sandwiches.
- Add nuts such as almonds, walnuts, pecans, pine nuts, and cashews to salads, relishes, pastas, and other foods. (Note: nuts can cause choking in children three years and younger. Use with caution.)
- Add lettuce, cucumbers, shredded carrots, celery, or sprouts to sandwiches.

- Add a teaspoon of flaxseed oil to salad dressings, yogurt, applesauce, and other foods to provide your child with the essential fatty acids necessary for healthy cell function and brain development.
- Cook vegetables in tomato sauce, purée, and pour over pasta.

Making the Most of your Laptop Lunch

Laptop Lunches have been designed for optimal flexibility. Use them with all four inner compartments in place if you're packing four different food items. Remove two inner compartments to form a larger compartment for a large sandwich or other main dish. Remove three inner compartments to accommodate an even larger main dish and fill the single inner compartment with a side dish. Keep in mind that your Laptop Lunch is deep enough for a sandwich, cut in half, to be stacked in one of the larger inner containers, leaving three compartments free for other food items such as a vegetable, fruit, and snack.

Use the sealable "wet" compartment for yogurt, cottage cheese, applesauce, or soup. Use the sealable sauce container for salad dressings, dips, relishes, and condiments. Include the fork and spoon as needed or use the utensil compartment for long, skinny food items such as steamed asparagus, green beans, carrot and celery sticks, or bread sticks.

Nutritional Balance

Choose a variety of foods each day. For example, you might want to choose one or two vegetables, a fruit, a protein, and a whole grain. Choose a different fruit and vegetable each day if possible. Have your children participate in the process of selecting the food by offering them alternatives for each category. Say, for example, "We have green beans, cucumbers, and broccoli in the house. Which one would you like to have in your lunch today?" If they've made the decision themselves, they're more likely to eat it.

Attractive Colors

Choose foods that vary in color by selecting foods that represent the colors of the rainbow. The American Academy of Pediatrics reminds us that offering a range of colorful fruits and vegetables provides a more varied and complete selection of nutrients. Invite your child to decide which food will go in each compartment.

Appealing Textures

Like us, children appreciate foods of different textures. Make an effort to choose foods that vary in texture; for example, choose a crunchy food such as a sliced apple, a smooth, wet food such as yogurt, and a dry, gooey food like an almond butter and banana sandwich on whole wheat bread. Exposing children to a variety of textures will help foster an appreciation for a wide range of foods.

Pleasing Shapes

Slice apples crosswise one day and quarter them another. Slice and cut them with small cookie-cutters for special occasions. Peel and section oranges one day and slice them into orange smiles or quarter them unpeeled another. Cut foods into interesting shapes when you can, for example, by making carrot flowers or using cookie cutters on pocket bread. Make cucumber rings or cucumber cups (see page 72) for variety. Look for interesting food-shaping gadgets at your local cooking store. Ask your children to help pick them out. Older children preparing their lunches can use these gadgets to make their own food more attractive.

Manageable Sizes

Younger children can be overwhelmed by large servings of food. Try cutting whole fruits into manageable finger foods or bite-sized pieces. Cut raw or steamed vegetables into smaller pieces and consider providing a nutritious dip. Buy baby carrots or cut larger carrots into carrot sticks or coins. For younger children pack a half sandwich cut in half again, or cut it into smaller cubes if your child prefers it that way.

When food is cut up, less is wasted. It is not uncommon to see a child take a few bites out of a whole apple and then toss the rest into the trash can. Whole apples are difficult to save for later. A cut up apple stored in a Laptop Lunch can be saved more easily because the child doesn't have to figure out how to wrap it back up again. Also, with cut up food, it's easier for a child to see that there's still something left to be saved.

Resist the temptation to completely fill all of your young child's Laptop Lunch compartments. Doing so might overwhelm her and cause her to overeat. Take your cues from your child, modifying what you pack as your child grows.

Dips, Dressings, and Condiments

Some children love dipping, pouring, and spreading their food. Use the Laptop Lunch dip container to this advantage. If you pack a green salad, pack the dressing "on the side" in the dip container. If your children are growing tired of carrot sticks, include their favorite dip. If your children complain that their sandwiches get soggy, pack two pieces of bread in one of the larger containers and a spread such as peanut butter or goat cheese in the dip container. Some children love making their own sandwiches at lunchtime.

Seasonal Specialties

Try to buy foods in season when they are most aromatic and flavorful. Your children will appreciate these seasonal treats much more when they haven't eaten them for months or even a whole year.

Temperature Control

If your children do not have access to a refrigerator at school, use a reusable ice pack in hot weather to keep foods cool and appetizing. If your children have access to a school microwave, consider packing soups and other warm foods in winter and on rainy days.

Wacky Wednesdays and Funny Fridays

Try adding surprises once in a while. Serve breakfast for lunch, for example, by packing eggs, a leftover pancake or waffle, a side of maple syrup, and some fresh fruit. Try wrapping your child's Laptop Lunch in a scarf, bandana, or cloth napkin and putting a silly picture or note inside. Look for books with tear-out lunch notes that you can slip into your child's lunchbox. *Lunch Box Letters: Writing Notes of Love and Encouragement to Your Children* by Carol Sperandeo and Bill Zimmerman, *Lunch Box Notes from Those Who Care* by Norm Caldwell, and *Lunch Box Notes* by SourceBooks, Inc. are just a few of the books available.

Wholesome Lunch Choices

The following is a quick-reference chart of lunch foods to choose from. If you're looking for fresh ideas, take a look. Read some of the suggestions to your children and ask them to make a list of foods they'd like to see in their lunchboxes. When you come up with ideas of your own, be sure to add them to the list for future reference. Try to choose a food from each category, keeping in mind that ingredients can be combined into something wonderful; for example, make a mini-fruit salad, a bagel with almond butter, or a vegetable medley of steamed green beans and carrots. If you're looking for more than a list of foods for inspiration, look ahead to the recipe section, which begins on page 61. See Appendix 4 for a 2-page nutritious food list that you can photocopy and post in the kitchen for easy reference.

Finally, keep in mind that some foods spoil more quickly than others. Make sure to provide adequate refrigeration in the form of an ice pack for foods that spoil easily, and avoid packing them on hot days.

Dried Fruits

apples   papaya
apricots   peaches
cranberries   pears
dates   pineapple
figs   prunes
mango   raisins
mixed fruit

Fresh Fruits

apples   mango
apricots   melon
Asian pears   nectarines
avocado   orange sections
bananas   papaya
blueberries   peaches
cherries   pears
dates   pineapple
figs   plums
grapefruit   raspberries
grapes   strawberries
kiwi   tomatoes

Raw Vegetables

bell peppers
broccoli
cabbage
carrots
cauliflower
celery
cucumbers

green beans
lettuce
mushrooms
shelling peas
snap peas
spinach
zucchini

Steamed Vegetables

asparagus
beets
bok choy
broccoli
brussels sprouts
cabbage
carrots
cauliflower
eggplant
green beans

potatoes
pumpkin
snap peas
soy beans (edamame)
spinach
squash
sweet potatoes
yams
zucchini

Other

mushrooms—sautéed or marinated
potatoes—baked, mashed, or pan-fried
seaweed—nori, wakame, hijiki

Proteins

beans (refried)
beans, dried (kidney, black, pinto, garbanzo, etc.)
beef (lean cuts only)
cheese (low-fat, lite, or soy)
chicken
cottage cheese (1%)
eggs (hard-boiled, scrambled, fried, or deviled)
egg salad
hot dogs (tofu or all natural chicken or turkey)
nut butters
nuts
pork
salmon
tofu (fresh or baked)
tuna*
turkey
yogurt (non-fat, low-fat, or soy)

*Due to high mercury levels, limit to once a week.

Grains

bagels
bread
buckwheat noodles
cereal, whole-grain,
    unsweetened
corn
couscous
crackers
lavash (flat bread)
oatmeal
pasta
pocket bread (pita)
polenta
popcorn (air-popped,
    not microwavable)
rice and pilaf
rice cakes
tortillas

Desserts and Treats

apple crisp
applesauce, unsweetened
banana rice pudding (page 75)
cookies (fig newtons, homemade oatmeal raisin)
fruit triangle treats (page 73)
granola
notes from home
oatmeal bars (page 74)
pretzels
stickers
trail mix (page 74)
yogurt with fruit

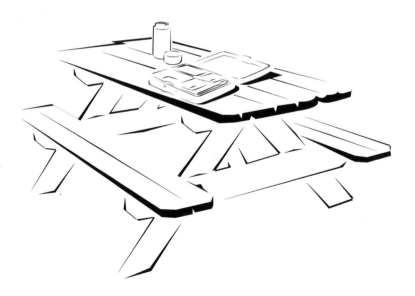

Smart Lunch Menus

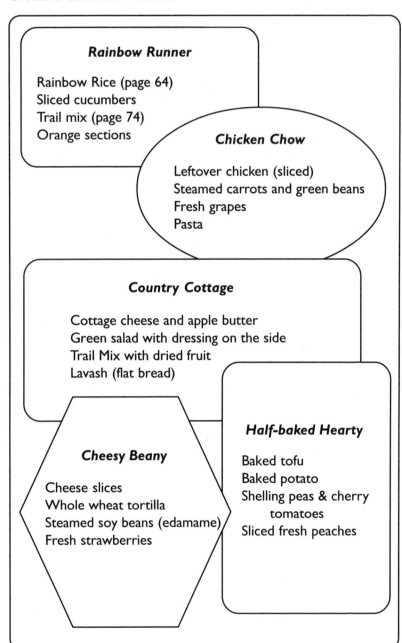

Rainbow Runner

Rainbow Rice (page 64)
Sliced cucumbers
Trail mix (page 74)
Orange sections

Chicken Chow

Leftover chicken (sliced)
Steamed carrots and green beans
Fresh grapes
Pasta

Country Cottage

Cottage cheese and apple butter
Green salad with dressing on the side
Trail Mix with dried fruit
Lavash (flat bread)

Cheesy Beany

Cheese slices
Whole wheat tortilla
Steamed soy beans (edamame)
Fresh strawberries

Half-baked Hearty

Baked tofu
Baked potato
Shelling peas & cherry
   tomatoes
Sliced fresh peaches

Chicken Polenta

Baked sliced chicken
Polenta Squares (page 70)
Carrots & broccoli
Mango slices

Quesadude

Quesadilla (page 64)
Green salad with
     dressing on the side
Sliced mango
Roasted almonds

Deviled Eggs and Yam

Deviled eggs
Whole-grain crackers
Steamed yams, beets, & zucchini
Sliced apples

Yolanda's Yogurt Surprise

Plain yogurt with maple syrup
Hearty Trail Mix (page 74)
Fresh kiwi and melon
Fresh carrots and bell peppers (green, red, yellow,
     and orange)

Monkephant Madness

Peanut butter and fresh
     banana sandwich
Yogurt
Steamed broccoli and
     cauliflower

Fruit and All

Fruit salad
Trail Mix (page 74)
Cottage cheese (1%)
Carrots and celery sticks

Pocket Power

Almond butter and honey
  pocket sandwich
Steamed carrots & asparagus
Sliced apples

Loafin' and Veggin'

Meatloaf sandwich
Dried pears
Steamed yams & snow peas

Eggventure

Egg salad sandwich
Fresh strawberries
Raw carrots and green beans

Chickle-Berry

Chicken salad sandwich
Pickles
Mixed strawberries,
  raspberries, and
  blueberries

Double Salad Wrap

Roll-up sandwich
Pasta salad
Fruit salad

Cal's Pal

Cheese, avocado and lettuce
  sandwich
Baked potato
Fresh cherries

Sea and Cee

Tuna sandwich
Cucumber Chain (page 72)
Sliced melon

Mexican Mango Madness

Bean and cheese Burrito
Sliced mango
Green salad with dressing on the side

Hearty-Breaky

Whole-wheat fruit pancakes
A hard-boiled or poached egg
100% maple syrup
Steamed Yams

Japanese Joy

Rice Triangles (page 71)
Cucumber Chain (page 72)
Sliced baked tofu
Sliced Asian pears

Pizza-Go-Round

Mini Whole Wheat Pizza Round topped with
cheese and vegetables (page 63)
Apple slices

Bagel Deluxe

Half bagel with lowfat cream cheese, fresh chopped dill,
smoked salmon, and a face made of raisin eyes,
cashew nose, and an apple smile.
Pan-fried potatoes & herbs
Applesauce

Using Leftovers

Don't forget about leftovers! Packing leftovers in your child's lunch can save you time and energy, and kids love them. When you're deciding what to cook for dinner, think about how you might incorporate leftovers into a lunch for the following day. Make a few extra servings for dinner and set them aside for the next day's lunch. While you're doing the after-dinner kitchen clean-up, place the Laptop Lunch on the counter. As you're putting away the food, pack some of the extras in the Laptop Lunch and refrigerate overnight. Here are a few ideas for making it work:

- If you make chicken breasts, prepare an extra serving and slice it for sandwiches the next day instead of purchasing deli lunch meat.
- If you're making a salad for dinner, slice some extra vegetables, such as cucumbers, carrots, bell peppers, and celery, or make an extra undressed salad directly in the Laptop Lunch. (Make extra dressing and pour it into the dip container.)
- While you're making dinner, boil some eggs. Pack them whole, make deviled eggs, or use them for egg salad.
- Make extra rice and use it to make Rainbow Rice (page 64) or Banana Rice Pudding (page 75).
- Make extra pasta, couscous, or rice and make side salads for lunch by cutting up vegetables and adding salad dressing.
- Grill extra vegetables and use them in sandwiches.
- Make an extra baked potato and pack it with nutritious toppings.

If you're worried that leftovers might seem less appealing the following day, consider packing them for lunch two days later, provided the food will remain fresh for an extra day.

Healthy Recipes

SANDWICH FILLINGS

Try some of these sandwich fillings in whole-wheat pocket bread, on whole-grain bread, bagels, crackers, English muffins, rice cakes or rolls, or try filling and rolling tortillas or lavash flat bread.

- Cheese, avocado, and sprouts
- Grilled cheese with cucumber or sprouts
- Shredded carrots, cucumbers, sunflower seeds, and avocado
- Leftover grilled vegetables (bell peppers, onions, mushrooms, eggplant, zucchini) with goat cheese or pesto sauce
- Cheddar or mozzarella cheese with apple slices
- Brie cheese with mustard and sprouts
- Baked tofu, tomato, sprouts or lettuce, and pesto sauce
- Leftover turkey loaf with tomatoes, and lettuce or sprouts
- Sliced leftover chicken or turkey, cranberry sauce, and lettuce
- Sliced leftover chicken or turkey, honey mustard, tomatoes, and lettuce or sprouts
- Sliced leftover beef with mayonnaise or horseradish, sliced tomato and cucumbers
- Chicken salad made with celery, lettuce, and tomato
- Tuna/cucumber/green pepper salad with tomato
- Salmon salad with lettuce or sprouts
- Shrimp salad with lettuce or sprouts
- Lowfat cream cheese, and smoked salmon (with tomato, fresh dill, and red onion)

VEGETARIAN MAIN DISHES

Mini Whole-Wheat Pizza Rounds

These mini-pizza rounds don't have to be round. They can be made into any shape, especially rectangles, which fit easily in a Laptop Lunch. Make them for dinner on Sunday afternoon and pack them for lunch on Monday. They're fun to make and fun to eat! Makes 5 servings.

Prep time: 25 minutes
Cook time: 25 minutes
Preheat oven to 475° F.

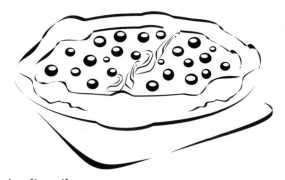

Ingredients:

DOUGH:

1 cup lukewarm water
1 package dry yeast
1 teaspoon salt
2 tablespoons extra-virgin olive oil
3-5 cups whole-wheat flour

TOPPINGS:

Extra-virgin olive oil
Fresh minced garlic
Fresh tomatoes, or high-quality pizza or spaghetti sauce
½ cup parmesan cheese, grated or shredded
8-16 ounces lite mozzarella cheese, grated
Fresh vegetables, such as onions, mushrooms, zucchini, bell peppers
(red, green, yellow and orange for color)
Fresh herbs, such as oregano, parsley, or basil

♦ In a large mixing bowl, combine water and yeast and stir well to dissolve.
♦ Let stand for 5 minutes.

- Add salt and olive oil, and beat well.
- Add 1 ½ cups whole-wheat flour and beat until smooth.
- Add 1 ½ cups more flour and stir as much as possible.
- Turn onto a floured board and kneed dough until smooth (about 5 minutes).
- Divide dough into five equal balls.
- With a rolling pin, roll to flatten, using additional flour to prevent sticking.
- Place on cookie sheets or pizza pans and let rise for 20 minutes.
- Brush lightly with olive oil, leaving an un-oiled border around the edge.
- Sprinkle with minced garlic and fresh herbs.
- Spoon tomato sauce onto surface of dough.
- Top with parmesan and mozzarella cheese.
- Add other toppings.
- Bake at 475° for 20 minutes or until cheese is melted, and crust is firm and golden.

Pizza Designs

Ladybugs: Make a round pizza and add toppings to resemble a ladybug. Put a line of bell pepper strips down the middle and add sliced black olives for spots.

Funny Faces: Make funny faces with the pizza toppings. Use green olives with pimentos for eyes, mushrooms for ears, red bell pepper slices for the mouth. Use broccoli, sliced red bell pepper, shredded zucchini, or marinated artichokes for the hair.

Deep Dish Pizza: Make the dough, roll it out, and mold it into a shallow baking dish. Add sauce, cheese, and toppings.

Pita Pizza: If you're short on time, forego the dough. Use pita bread or an English muffin instead. Add sauce, cheese, and toppings. Heat and serve. If your children have a microwave at school, pack the fixings and let them assemble it there.

Quesadilla with Attitude

Quesadillas are an all-time favorite. They're quick to prepare and fun to eat. Experiment by adding some of these other healthy ingredients after cooking: mango or peach salsa, cooked brown rice and refried beans, sliced or mashed avocado, shredded carrot, shredded lettuce, or alfalfa sprouts. Ask your child to provide you with additional ideas. Soy cheese may be substituted for cheese.

Spread thinly cut cheese slices or grated cheese on one half of a tortilla. Place it on a heated griddle or on a metal sheet in the toaster oven. Heat until the cheese melts. Remove from the oven. Place sliced avocado and any other toppings on top of cheese. Fold in half along cheese line. Cut into wedges. Serve with mild salsa.

If your children have access to a microwave, they can reheat their quesadillas at school.

Rainbow Rice

This dish can be made with whatever vegetables you happen to have in the house. Try to choose vegetables that represent the colors of the rainbow! This 20-minute recipe is a great way to use leftover rice.

Choose your vegetables. Cabbage, onions, bell peppers, zucchini, broccoli, spinach, carrots, and celery work well. Prepare 5 cups of diced vegetables. Make 2 cups of rice or use leftover rice. Add a small amount of olive oil to a large frying pan or wok and scramble an egg. Add the vegetables and sauté until vegetables are soft but not limp. Add the rice and mix thoroughly. Season with one of the following:

- soy sauce, pepper, and sesame oil
- 2 tablespoons lemon juice, 2 teaspoons cumin, and 1/3 cup parsley
- ½ cup fresh cilantro and ½ cup Mexican salsa
- your favorite marinade

Literary Lunch: Add ½ cup cooked whole-grain multi-colored alphabet pasta. Children will love searching for the letters while they eat.

SIDE DISHES

Potato Pancakes

Kids love pancakes and potato pancakes are no exception. This is a great opportunity for kids to use the much beloved cheese grater. Serve potato pancakes for dinner and pack the extras for lunch. Serve with applesauce. They're quick and yummy. Makes eight 3-inch pancakes.

Prep time: 15 minutes
Cook time: 15-20 minutes

Ingredients:

2 cups grated potato
½ cup grated onion (optional)
2 eggs, beaten
¼ cup whole-wheat flour
¼ teaspoon salt
Applesauce, apple butter, yogurt (optional)

Oil for cooking

- ◆ Coarsely grate the potatoes and onions into a large mixing bowl or shred in a food processor.
- ◆ Squeeze out excess liquid.
- ◆ Add the beaten eggs and stir to mix thoroughly.
- ◆ Add the whole-wheat flour and salt and stir well.
- ◆ Add a small amount of oil to a nonstick frying pan.
- ◆ Cook on medium-low heat until pancakes have browned on the bottom. (Do not overcook.)
- ◆ Flip the pancakes and cook on the other side until they are cooked through.
- ◆ Remove from pan and blot with paper towels, if needed.
- ◆ Serve with applesauce, apple butter, or yogurt.

Variation: Substitute some of the potatoes with grated apple, cheddar cheese, carrots, zucchini, or parsnips.

Asian Pasta Salad

This flavorful salad is a great way to get vegetables into your kids—and your kids into vegetables! Makes 6 servings.

Prep time: 15 minutes
Cook time: about 10 minutes

Ingredients:

8 oz. of your children's favorite pasta
1 cup broccoli, cut into bite-size pieces
*1 ½ cups green beans, sugar snap peas, cabbage, or zucchini, cut
  into bite-size pieces*
¾ cup carrots cut into thin 1-inch strips
1 clove minced garlic (optional)
2 tablespoons sesame oil
2 tablespoons soy sauce
2 tablespoons sesame seeds
2 tablespoons chopped fresh cilantro
½ cup bean sprouts
Water for boiling pasta

- Boil pasta in a large pot until it is half-cooked.
- Add all vegetables (except bean sprouts) and boil until the pasta is *al dente* and the vegetables are tender.
- Drain and place in a large bowl.
- Make a salad dressing by mixing together the garlic, sesame oil, and soy sauce.
- Add the sesame seeds, cilantro, bean sprouts and salad dressing to the pasta and toss well.

Variation: If your family likes spicy food, add some hot Chinese oil and freshly chopped scallions.

Cold Pasta with Peanut Butter Dressing

This cold pasta dish is an instant hit with little (and big) peanut butter lovers. Makes 6 servings.

Prep time: 20-25 minutes
Cook time: about 15 minutes (+ refrigeration time if serving cold)

Ingredients:

8 oz. of your children's favorite pasta
1 cup each of shredded red and green cabbage
1 carrot cut into thin 1-inch strips
2 tablespoons rice vinegar
2 tablespoons soy sauce
1/3 cup peanut butter
1 clove minced or crushed garlic, or to taste
½ cucumber, diced
4 tablespoons chopped fresh cilantro
¼ cup chopped scallions or red onion (optional)
¾ cups bean sprouts (optional)
Water for boiling pasta

- Boil pasta until it is half-cooked.
- Add the shredded cabbage and carrot strips to the pasta and cook until the pasta is *al dente* and the vegetables are tender but not mushy.
- Drain in a colander and rinse with cold water to prevent sticking and to cool, if desired.
- Transfer to a large bowl.
- Make a salad dressing by mixing or blending together the garlic, rice vinegar, soy sauce, and peanut butter.
- Add the salad dressing to the pasta mixture and toss well.
- Add the diced cucumber, cilantro, scallions, and bean sprouts and toss again.
- Chill or eat warm.

Garden Party Pasta Salad

Tomatoes, basil, and mozzarella can make any day feel like a summer holiday! Makes 4-5 servings.

Prep time: 20-30 minutes
Cook time: about 10 minutes

Ingredients:

8 oz. of your children's favorite pasta
4 large ripe tomatoes, diced
½ cup fresh chopped basil
1 clove garlic (optional)
4 ounces mozzarella cheese, diced
¼ cup kalamata olives (optional)
3 tablespoons olive oil
Pine nuts (optional)
Salt and pepper to taste
Water for boiling pasta

- ◆ Boil the pasta until *al dente*.
- ◆ In a large bowl, combine the tomatoes, basil, garlic, mozzarella cheese, kalamata olives, and olive oil.
- ◆ Drain the pasta and add to the tomato mixture.
- ◆ Toss gently, and garnish with fresh basil leaves and pine nuts.

Vegetable Stir-Fry

This dish is loaded with color. To make it even more appealing, pack it for lunch with some extra sauce on the side. Makes 4-5 servings.

Prep time: 15 minutes
Cook time: about 15 minutes

Ingredients:

2 tablespoons olive oil
2 cloves garlic, minced
1 tablespoon grated fresh ginger (optional)
½ cup chopped raw meat such as salmon, chicken (optional)
5 cups chopped fresh vegetables of your choice (Onions,
*   mushrooms, zucchini, green beans, cabbage, spinach, chard,*
*   kale, tofu, bell peppers, eggplant, broccoli, asparagus, snow*
*   peas, bok choy, carrots, and cauliflower all work well.)*
Soy sauce, to taste
Sesame seed oil, to taste
Salt and pepper to taste

- Chop all vegetables and meat (optional) into bite-size pieces.
- Pour olive oil into a non-stick frying pan and heat.
- Add minced garlic and cook on medium-low until pungent.
- Add grated ginger, if desired.
- Add meat, if you are using it.
- Add chopped vegetables, starting with those that will take longest to cook, such as onions, carrots, and bell peppers, and progressing to those that will require the least amount of cooking.
- Season with soy sauce, sesame seed oil, salt and pepper to taste.
- Remove from heat.
- Serve over brown rice or whole-wheat couscous.

Polenta Squares

These easy-to-make, easy-to-eat yellow polenta squares will add a bit of color and a blast of fun to any lunch. Make them for dinner and pack the leftovers for lunch. Top with marinara sauce or salsa, grated lite mozzarella cheese, and sliced olives. Makes 8 servings.

Prep time: 5 minutes
Cook time: 30 minutes (+ one hour to chill, if serving cold)

Ingredients:

4 cups water or stock
1 cup coarse yellow cornmeal or grits
1 teaspoon salt
1-2 tablespoons olive oil

◆ Bring the water to a boil, and add the salt and oil.
◆ Slowly add the cornmeal, stirring constantly with a wire whisk.
◆ When the mixture starts to boil, turn the heat to low.
◆ Stir every few minutes until the grain has swelled and the mixture has thickened (about 30 minutes).
◆ Turn off the heat.
◆ Pour polenta into a baking dish and smooth the surface with a large spoon. (The polenta should be ¾- to 1-inch deep.)
◆ If serving warm, bake for 15 minutes at 350° F.
◆ If serving cold, cover and refrigerate for at least one hour.
◆ Cut into squares, top with marinara sauce, grated mozzarella, and sliced black olives.

Garlic Toast

Brush bread lightly with olive oil. Sprinkle chopped parsley and minced garlic on top. Sprinkle with paprika, if desired. Toast in toaster oven (or oven) until golden brown.

Use as sandwich bread or pack as a separate item.
For croutons, cut into ¾-inch cubes.

Rice Triangles

This American adaptation of a Japanese favorite makes a delicious lunch treat. They're easy to pack and easy to hold. They also make a great, nutritious class snack for parties and special occasions. Makes 12 pieces.

Prep time: 20 minutes
Cook time: about 45 minutes

Ingredients:

3 cups (whole-grain) sushi rice
½ cup rice vinegar
1 teaspoon salt
¼ cup sugar
2 tablespoons sweet sake or mirin
3 tablespoons sesame seeds
6 sheets nori seaweed
Water for cooking rice

- ◆ Wash rice, drain, and cook as directed.
- ◆ While rice is cooking, prepare vinegar sauce by mixing together the vinegar, salt, sugar and sake or mirin and set aside.
- ◆ Remove the rice from the heat.
- ◆ Add vinegar sauce and toss to mix.
- ◆ Add sesame seeds and toss again.
- ◆ Allow rice to cool.
- ◆ Wet hands and mold rice mixture into 1-inch thick triangles with 2 ½-inch sides.
- ◆ Cut nori sheets in half and wrap each rice triangle in one half sheet.

For variety, shape the rice into different shapes. Try logs, spheres, cubes, and pyramids. Instead of wrapping shapes in seaweed, as a variation, cut seaweed into 1-inch ribbons and wrap around the edges of the rice triangles.

Cucumber Cups

♦ Cut the end from an unpeeled cucumber.
♦ Starting about two inches from the end of the cucumber, make a slanted cut from the outside of the cucumber toward the center.
♦ Make two more of these cuts, and take out the cone shaped center.
♦ If you want a larger cup, scoop out more of the inside of the cucumber with a spoon.
♦ To make additional cups, first cut off the cone shaped part of the cucumber and start with a flat end once again.
♦ Stuff the cucumber cups with egg, tuna, salmon or chicken salad, or fill with salad dressing and use as a dipping bowl for other vegetables.

Cucumber Chains

♦ Cut a cucumber into 2-inch long cylinders.
♦ Remove the core with a paring knife.
♦ Slice it into ¼-inch rings.
♦ Make a slit in every other ring.
♦ Link the rings together
    to form a chain.

DESSERTS AND SPECIAL TREATS

Fruit Triangle Treats

Our kids love eating these fruit wedges as a breakfast treat and as a lunch treat the following day. Try them with other types of fruit, such as peaches, pears, or blueberries, or sprinkle with granola, sunflower seeds, or sesame seeds.

Prep time: 15 minutes
Cook time: 30 minutes
Preheat the oven to 375° F.

Ingredients:

*4 medium apples, peeled, cored,
        and sliced into ¼ inch slices.*
*1 tablespoon walnut or other
        high-quality oil*
1 tablespoon lemon juice
1 tablespoon honey
2 teaspoons ground cinnamon
3 eggs
½ cup milk or soy milk
½ cup whole-wheat flour

- ◆ Pour the walnut oil into a 10-inch pie pan and spread to cover bottom.
- ◆ Pour the lemon juice, honey, and 1 teaspoon of the cinnamon over the apples and mix.
- ◆ In a medium-size bowl beat the eggs well.
- ◆ Add the milk or soy milk.
- ◆ Combine the whole-wheat flour and the cinnamon.
- ◆ Add whole-wheat mixture to egg mixture and stir to form a batter.
- ◆ Pour the batter into the oiled pie pan.
- ◆ Place the apple slices on top of the batter, covering the surface. (The apples will sink into the batter.)
- ◆ Bake at 375° F for 30 minutes or until the batter is firm and the apples are cooked.

Oatmeal Bars

These oatmeal bars are a great alternative to many similar prepackaged products. Freeze some for future use. Preheat oven to 350° F.

Prep time: 15 minutes
Cook time: 15 minutes

Ingredients:

3 cups whole oats
2/3 cup whole-wheat flour
½ teaspoon baking soda
½ teaspoon salt
1 teaspoon ground cinnamon

1/3 cup honey
1/3 cup walnut oil
1 egg, beaten
3 tablespoons orange juice or water
1 teaspoon vanilla extract

- Combine oatmeal, flour, baking soda, salt, and cinnamon together in a large bowl and mix well.
- In a separate bowl, combine honey, oil, egg, orange juice (or water), and vanilla extract. Mix thoroughly.
- Combine the dry and wet ingredients and mix again.
- Using a spatula, press mixture firmly onto a lightly oiled cookie sheet, forming one large rectangle about 1/3 inch thick.
- Smooth the edges with the edge of the spatula.
- Bake at 350° F for 12-15 minutes, until light brown and firm.
- Remove from oven and cool.
- Using a sharp knife, cut the large rectangle into smaller 1½-inch by 3½-inch rectangles.

Trail Mix

Make your own trail mix by trying various combinations of the following:

peanuts	pecans	raisins and other dried fruit
almonds	pretzels	semi-sweet chocolate chips
cashews	sunflower seeds	unsweetened shredded coconut
walnuts	healthy cereal	

Banana Rice Pudding

Kids love this wholesome version of an age-old treat! Make extra brown rice for dinner and use it to make this recipe for lunch. Makes 4 servings.

Prep time: 5 minutes, if rice is already cooked
Cook time: 25 minutes

Ingredients:

1 medium banana
¼ cup water
2 tablespoons honey or maple syrup
1 teaspoon vanilla extract
½ teaspoon ground cinnamon
2 cups cooked brown rice
1 cup nonfat milk (or soy milk)

♦ In a medium-size saucepan, combine the banana, water, honey, vanilla, and cinnamon.
♦ Bring the mixture to a boil and stir.
♦ Reduce the heat and simmer for 5 minutes or until soft but not mushy.
♦ Add the rice and milk and mix well.
♦ Bring to a boil again and simmer for 10 minutes more, stirring occasionally.

For variety, add raisins and walnuts, or seasonal fresh fruit such as peeled and diced peaches, apples, or apricots instead of banana.

For additional recipes, visit our Web site at www.laptoplunches.com.

Waste-Free Lunch Programs

Sharon Yntema in her book *Vegetarian Children* explains that children need to develop an awareness of dietary issues outside of the home so that they can understand nutrition in a larger cultural context. This greater awareness, she asserts, should begin at school where parents and teachers can work together to teach children about social responsibility and the relationship between nutrition and the environment.

In an effort to teach children about the environmental impacts of their own food choices, many schools have implemented waste-free lunch programs. If your school does not already have one, and you are interested in starting one, you have some resources available to you. Search the Internet to find out what other schools are doing. Visit www.wastefreelunches.org for practical ideas. Contact state and local agencies to find out what materials and services are available. Check to see if you can qualify for a county or state waste-reduction grant. If your school has a life lab program, talk to the life lab instructor. He or she may know about what's going on in other schools and might have access to teaching materials. Check your library for additional resources.

Meanwhile, it's important to keep in mind that a waste-free lunch program will most likely succeed if it does the following:

- Involves parents and faculty as well as students
- Reaches a broad number of students in all grades
- Provides an incentive program for students
- Encompasses both environmental studies and nutrition
- Provides a means for parents to comply easily, for example, by providing them with sound nutrition information, convenient lunch food suggestions, and reusable lunch containers
- Approaches the topic in a variety of ways, for example, using art, music and film, taking field trips, inviting guest speakers, conducting experiments, and writing reports
- Involves age-appropriate hands-on learning activities like making collages, conducting trash audits, sorting and categorizing trash, graphing trash audit results, taking fieldtrips to the dump and/or recycling facility, and integrating the program with the school life lab program

Other Waste-Saving Ideas

- Reduce, refuse, recycle, reuse.

- Plant your own organic garden.

- Start a compost pile.

- Refuse packaging. Take your own grocery bags, plastic produce bags, and bulk containers when you go shopping.

- Buy recycled and used products at second-hand shops, yard sales, and recycle stores.

- Turn off lights, televisions, computers, stereos, and other appliances when not in use.

- Instead of driving, ride your bike, walk, or take public transportation.

- Carpool when you can.

- Report water drips or leaks that you find in public places.

- Carry a handkerchief in your pocket or purse. Use it to dry your hands in public restrooms instead of using paper towels. (If you don't have your handkerchief, limit yourself to just one paper towel.)

- Wrap gifts in reusable gift bags instead of wrapping paper.

- Take your own reusable container to restaurants for leftovers. Better yet, take your children's laptop lunches and pack them with leftovers for school the following day.

Resources for Children and Teens

Carlson, Laurie. *Ecoart.* Charlotte, VT: Williamson Publishing, 1993.

Dr. Suess. *The Lorax.* New York: Random House, 1971.

The Earth at Risk Environmental Video Series. *Recycling.* Cynwyd, PA: Sclessinger Video Productions, 1993.

The Earth Works Group. *The Recycler's Handbook.* Berkeley: Earth Works Press, 1990.

Elkington, John, et al. *Going Green: A Kid's Handbook to Saving the Planet.* New York: Puffin Books, 1990.

Gutnik, Martin J. *Recycling: Learning the Four R's.* Hillside, NJ: Enslow Publishers, Inc., 1993.

Krizmanic, Judy. *A Teen's Guide to Going Vegetarian.* New York: Puffin Books, 1994.

Miles, Betty. *Save the Earth.* New York: Alfred A. Knopf, 1991.

Rockwell, Harlow. *The Compost Heap.* Garden City, NY: Doubleday, 1974.

Ross, Kathy. *Every Day is Earth Day.* Brookfield, CN: The Millbrook Press, 1995.

Seltzer, Meyer. *Here Comes the Recycling Truck.* Morton Grove, IL: Albert Whitman & Company, 1992.

VanCleave, Janice. *Food and Nutrition for Every Kid: Easy Activities that Make Learning Science Fun.* New York: John Wiley and Sons, Inc., 1999.

Wilcox, Charlotte and Jerry Bushey. *Trash!* Minneapolis, MN: Carolfhoda Books, Inc., 1988.

Cookbooks for Nutritious Eating

Brown, Edward Espe. *The Tassajara Bread Book*. Boston: Shambhala Publications, Inc., 1986.

Callan, Ginny. *Beyond the Moon Cookbook*. New York: HarperCollins Publishers, 1996.

Callan, Ginny. *Horn of the Moon Cookbook*. New York: HarperPerennial, 1987.

Drennan, Matthew. *Fast Vegetarian Food*. New York: Southwater, 2001.

Elliot, Rose. *The Complete Vegetarian Cuisine*. New York: Pantheon Books, 1988.

Elliot, Rose. *Vegetarian Fast Food*. New York: Random House, Inc., 1994.

Jaffrey, Madhur. *World Vegetarian*. New York: Clarkson Potter/Publishers, 1999.

Katzen, Mollie. *The Moosewood Cookbook*. Berkeley, CA: Ten Speed Press, 1992.

Lair, Cynthia. *Feeding the Whole Family*. Seattle: Moon Smile Press, 1997.

McCartney, Linda. *Linda McCartney On Tour*. Boston: Little, Brown and Company, 1998.

Shulman, Martha Rose. *The Vegetarian Feast*. New York: Harper & Row Publishers, 1979.

Spieler, Marlena. *Vegetarian Pasta*. San Francisco: HarperCollins Publishers, 1995.

Thomas, Anna. *The New Vegetarian Epicure*. New York: Alfred A. Knopf, 1996.

Trelvar, Brigid. *Healthy Soy: Cooking with Soybeans for Health and Vitality*. Boston: Periplus Editions, Ltd., 2002.

Appendix 1: Family Discussion Worksheet

The following worksheet is designed to help you make changes that will reduce waste and improve your family's eating habits. Set up a meeting with all members of the family to discuss the reasons for the change and to devise a plan for implementing the changes.

Part I: Waste Reduction

In a typical week, how many of the following items does your family as a whole take to school and work?

A Look at Our Family Lunches	How many per week?	Can we reduce?
Plastic bags		Yes / No
Prepackaged food items		Yes / No
Disposable drink containers		Yes / No
Plastic forks and spoons		Yes / No
Paper napkins		Yes / No
Paper bags		Yes / No
As a family what can we do to reduce lunch waste?		

Part II: Nutrition

In a typical week, how many of the following items do family members (in total) take to school or work?

A Look at Our Family Lunches	How many per week?	Can we reduce?
Non-fruit desserts		Yes / No
High-sugar non-dessert items		Yes / No
High-sugar drinks		Yes / No
White varieties of grain products		Yes / No
Meat products		Yes / No
Processed food items		Yes / No
High-fat snack foods		Yes / No
High sodium snack foods		Yes / No.

What can we do to improve the nutritional value of the food we pack? Are we eating at least five fruits and vegetables daily?

Part III: Implementation Plan

Look at Parts I and II. Make a plan for implementing changes. Begin by prioritizing the changes you have decided to make and listing them in order below. Then make an implementation schedule agreed upon by the whole family.

Changes	Implementation Dates

Appendix 2: The Star Incentive Program

If a waste-free lunch program is implemented at school and supported at home, most children will comply easily and with enthusiastic support. However, some children may resist the change. If you are facing this challenge, try using the Star Incentive Program.

- First ask your child why he or she does not want to participate. Validate the child's feelings, and try to accommodate any requests that are reasonable and acceptable to you.
- Next, talk with your child about the importance of good health and caring for the environment.
- Ask your child to help plan a lunch menu program. If your children are old enough, and if they aren't doing so already, find out if they would like to help prepare their lunches.
- If your child is worried about being the only kid at school with a waste-free lunch, you may want to talk with other parents about joining you in your endeavor to reduce waste, or consider instituting a waste-free lunch program at the school. If reducing waste is a community effort, children will accept it and may even become enthusiastic supporters.
- To use the Star Incentive Program you will first need to purchase star (or other) stickers. Increase motivation by allowing your child to pick them out.
- At the beginning of each month, photocopy the blank Star Incentive Calendar provided on the next page. (More than one child can use the same calendar. Photocopy the second month onto the back of the first to save paper.)
- Reward your children with a sticker for each day that they agree to take a waste-free lunch to school.
- When they have accumulated a certain number of stickers, allow them to pick out a special treat, such as a trip to the movies or to a play, or arrange a play date with a friend who, because of distance, you would not normally make the effort to get together with. An outing to a special place, such as a favorite park, an amusement park, a children's museum, or other place of interest, might also motivate them.

- You can give the stickers to the children in the morning, when they return from school, or put them in their lunchbox as a lunchtime surprise.

The Star Incentive Calendar

Monday	Tuesday	Wednesday	Thursday	Friday

Appendix 3: The HealthPoint System

The HealthPoint System has been designed as an incentive for children to eat a more nutritious diet.

- Begin by explaining the program to your children. Look together at the HealthPoint Chart on the next page and discuss each category as a family. Decide on a collective family point goal and choose a special family reward for achieving that goal. Some possibilities include renting a family video, or going to a museum, play, concert, or family movie. Take a hike together, plan a special meal together, or go out to a restaurant that serves nutritious food.
- Each person in the family receives one point for each nutritious food eaten, four points for each day without junk food, and four points for each day that they are physically active.
- Encourage all family members to keep track of what they eat and to encourage and praise one another.
- Continue the program until you feel that everyone in the family is working together to eat well.

HealthPoint Chart

Food Choices	Points	Monday	Tuesday	Wednesday	Thursday	Friday
Servings of whole grains	1 point each					
Servings of fruits	1 point each					
Servings of vegetables	1 point each					
Up to five servings of protein	1 point each					
Water instead of sweetened drinks	1 point each					
Six cups of water or more	1 point each					
No junk food	4 points/day					
Daily exercise	4 points/day					
	TOTAL					

Appendix 4: Quick Reference Lunch Ideas

Breads	Spreads & Condiments	Fillings
bagel	almond butter	carrots (shredded)
baguette	apple butter	cheese (lowfat)
bread sticks	avocado (mashed)	chicken
crackers	banana (mashed)	chicken salad
English muffin	brie cheese	egg salad
focaccia	cashew butter	hard-boiled egg
lavash bread	cream cheese (lowfat)	nitrite-free hot dogs
pita bread	goat cheese	lettuce
pizza bread	honey	shrimp salad
rice cakes	hummus	sliced avocado
rolls	jam (spreadable fruit)	sliced cucumber
sandwich bread	ketchup	smoked salmon
tortillas	mayonnaise/mustard	sprouts
	peanut butter	tofu
	pesto	tuna salad
	pizza or tomato sauce	turkey
	pumpkin butter	
	tahini (sesame paste)	

Fruits (Dried and Fresh)		
apples	figs	melon
apricots	grapefruit	nectarines
Asian pears	grapes	orange sections
avocado	kiwi	peaches
bananas	mango	pineapple
blueberries	papaya	plums
cherries	pears	raspberries
cranberries	prunes	strawberries
dates	raisins	tomatoes

Vegetables

asparagus
beets
bell peppers
bok choy
broccoli
brussels sprouts
cabbage
carrots
cauliflower
celery
cucumbers
eggplant
green beans

green salad
lettuce
mushrooms
potatoes
seaweed (nori, wakame, hijiki)
shelling peas
snap peas
soy beans (edamame)
spinach
squash
sweet potatoes
yams
zucchini

Treats

apple crisp
applesauce, unsweetened
baked chips with salsa
Banana Rice Pudding (page 75)
dried fruit
fruit bar
fruit leather
Fruit Triangle Treats (page 73)
granola

homemade cookies
notes from home
Oatmeal Bars (page 74)
popcorn (air-popped)
pretzels
stickers
Trail Mix (page 74)
vanilla yogurt with fruit

Other

baked tofu
bean burrito
cottage cheese with fruit
Garlic Toast (page 70)
polenta with pizza sauce & cheese

pasta
rice
couscous
oatmeal
bulghar

Selected Bibliography

American Academy of Pediatrics. *Pediatric Nutrition Handbook,* Fourth Edition. Elk Grove Village, IL: American Academy of Pediatrics, 1998.

Bell, Dawson. "Michigan's Lieutenant Governor Wants Canada to Keep Its Garbage." *Detroit Free Press* 13 Nov 2001.

Caldwell, Norm. *Lunch Box Notes from Those Who Care.* Taylor, MI. Mother's Publishing House, 1998.

Campbell, Susan and Todd Winant. *Healthy School Lunch Action Guide.* Santa Cruz, CA: EarthSave Foundation, 1994.

Carless, Jennifer. *Taking Out the Trash.* Washington, D.C.: Island Press, 1992.

The Colombia University College of Physicians and Surgeons Complete Guide to Early Child Care. New York: Crown Publishers, Inc., 1990.

Dietz, William H. and Loraine Stern (Ed.). *Guide to Your Child's Nutrition.* New York: Random House, 1999.

Haynes, Linda. *The Vegetarian Lunchbasket.* Willow Springs, MO: Nucleus Publications, 1990.

Hunter, Beatrice Trum. "Revamping School Meal Programs." *Consumer's Research Magazine* Nov 1998: 24+.

Hunter, Beatrice Trum. *Consumer's* "Upgrading School Lunches." *Research Magazine* Oct 1996: 8.

"Is your kid failing lunch?" *Consumer Reports* Sept. 1998: 49.

Jacobson, Michael F., et. al. *Safe Food: Eating Wisely in a Risky World.* Venice, CA: Living Planet Press, 1991.

Lacy, Richard W. *Hard to Swallow.* Cambridge, MA: Cambridge University Press, 1994.

Lair, Cynthia. *Feeding the Whole Family.* Seattle, WA: Moon Smile Press, 1997.

Lappé, Frances Moore. *Diet for a Small Planet.* New York: Ballantine Books, 1982.

Lutz, Steven M. and Jay Hirschman. "School Lunch Reform: Minimal Market Impacts From Providing Healthier Meals." *Food Review* Jan-Apr 1998: 28+.

Moll, Lucy. *The Vegetarian Child.* New York: The Berkley Publishing Group, 1997.

Moloney, Paul. "Garbage Contract Lands in Michigan." *Toronto Star* 5 Dec 2001, 3.

Nussbaum, Alex. "New York City Dumps Disposal Problem on New Jersey." *The Record* 10 Sept 2001.

Peavy, Linda S. and Andrea L Pagenkopf. *Grow Healthy Kids!: A Parents' Guide to Sound Nutrition from Birth through Teens.* New York: Grosset & Dunlap, 1980.

Robbins, John. *Diet for a New America.* Walpole, NH: Stillpoint Publishing, 1987.

Sears, William, and Martha Sears *The Family Nutrition Book.* New York: Little Brown and Company, 1999.

Simon, Michele. "Vegetarian Action: Innovative School Lunch Programs Gaining Success." *Vegetarian Journal* 28 Feb 1999: 35.

SourceBooks, Inc. *Lunch Box Notes.* Napperville, IL, 2000.

Sperandeo, Carol and Bill Zimmerman. *Lunch Box Letters: Writing Notes of Love and Encouragement to Your Children.* Buffalo, NY: Firefly Books, 2000.

Springen, Karen. "Lunchbox Magic." *Vegetarian Times.* Sept 1993: 28-30.

U.S. Dietary Guidelines, Fifth Edition 2000, U.S. Department of Agriculture and U.S. Department of Health and Human Services, Home and Garden Bulletin, No. 32.

Winter, Ruth. *A Consumer's Dictionary of Food Additives.* New York: Three Rivers Press, 1999.

Wood, Rebecca. *The New Whole Foods Encyclopedia: A Comprehensive Resource for Healthy Eating.* New York: The Penguin Group, 1999.

Yntema, Sharon K. *Vegetarian Children.* Ithaca, NY: McBooks Press, 1987.

Index

V

vegetable stir-fry 69
vegetables 14, 16, 23, 53, 88

W

waste reduction 7-8, 29
waste-free lunch programs 76
waste-saving ideas 77
water 26, 27, 47
whole grains 23, 32

Y

yogurt cultures 36-37

Laptop Lunches

Visit our Web site at *www.laptoplunches.com*.